Rm 535

▶ Decoding Strategies

Decoding B1
Student Book

Siegfried Engelmann • Linda Meyer • Linda Carnine
• Wesley Becker • Julie Eisele • Gary Johnson

SRA
McGraw-Hill

Columbus, Ohio

A Division of The McGraw·Hill Companies

Table of Contents

SRA/McGraw-Hill

A Division of The McGraw-Hill Companies

2002 Imprint
Copyright © 1999 by SRA/McGraw-Hill.

Send all inquiries to:
SRA/McGraw-Hill
8787 Orion Place
Columbus, Ohio 43240-4027

Printed in the United States of America.

ISBN 0-02-674779-0

5 6 7 8 9 VHJ 04 03 02 01

PHOTO CREDITS   Cover Photo: KS Studios

1   m f l s n

2   j k t d p

3   i a e ee

(a) pit see at meet am keep

(b) jam and lid tap pan fill

(c) dad seem if sits feeds is

4   th that the this teeth

5   cap clip pick cat clap tack

6

1. Did that man slip?

2. Can the cat sleep in a lap?

3. Clip the plant and keep the tip.

4. A cat can see it is dim.

5. At last, I can sleep.

6. Keep the seeds in this sack.

[1]

1. Did the ant land in a sand pit?

2. Pick a cap that fits this can.

3. Slip this stick in the pack.

4. Is a man as fast as a cat?

5. Did that man see the last plan?

6. Fill this flat pan.

[2]

1   l   s   m   f   n

2   p   d   k   j   t

3   e   i   a   ee
(a) sit   seem   cat   need   mad   seen
(b) hat   and   fit   cap   fill   tan
(c) did   seed   it   sit   feeds   is

4   th   this   than   math   teeth

5   can   clip   pick   stick   clap   pack

6

1. That man sleeps in a tree.

2. Did the ant sit in sand?

3. Fill that can and keep it.

4. Can I keep that seed sack?

5. Dad can see the cats sleep.

6. Stick that pan in this pack.

[1]

1. Did the lamp seem dim?

2. I need a cap that fits in this pack.

3. Did that tack stick the cat?

4. Plant this seed in sand.

5. The ant sat in a back pack.

6. Is that jam in the can?

[2]

1 m d f j n
p l s k t

---

2 a e i ee

---

3 r w g h

---

4 u o

up sun no

cup so run cut

---

5 th sh or

6 with ship than for
wish torn math cash
corn sheet store

7
(a) to do slip sand last fits
(b) he fun gas go deer us
(c) hill drink flag plant rats
(d) rams has three wish will milk

8
1. Last week, we had fun at the track meet.

2. She can go with us.

3. Is that street as slick as it seems?

4. Can he go to the store with us?

5. Will that truck slip in the sand?

6. He had a sack, a pack, and a cap for a can.

[1]

1. This is the last store we will go to.

2. Fill this can with gas.

3. That truck can go as fast as a deer.

4. If she is sick, I will go to the drug store.

5. At last, she has a cat that she can keep.

6. She had a plan for the trip.

[2]

1 n f d j r
s l k t p

_____

2 e i ee a

_____

3 h w g r

_____

4 o u

cut sun no go
so cup fun

_____

5 sh th or

6 wish with ship torn
than math cash
corn for store sheet

_____

7 (a) to gas do last sand milk
(b) he us fun go drink meet
(c) kill flag fit plant sink
(d) rats ship three fish will

8

1. Will the truck go to the seed store?

2. I need to keep that pack for the trip.

3. Did she pick a plant that is green?

4. Cats can drink milk.

5. If I feel sick, I can't go.

6. Three sheep sleep with a deer.

[1]

1. Can we go to the drug store?

2. I will fill this gas can.

3. See the flag at the truck plant.

4. Will that milk last us for a week?

5. I wish I had three cats.

6. Fill the gas tank in that green truck.

[2]

1
d l t s m f
n g h r w

2
o e a i u ee

3
o on hop rod
shop rock got

4
tree flap drip plan
seems track clock steep
trap stop creek flag
win truck hand sleep

5
ol old told colt gold

6
for fold wish with ship
teeth more shop cold
sheets store that rash

7
do to said
was give have

8

1. The man said, "We can go on a short trip."

2. She said, "Give me the green clip."   3. "We will win the meet," he said.

9

1. I have seen that old truck.

2. Was she at the store with him?

3. We have a plan for a fun trip.

4. His clock did not run.

5. Give me a hand with this sack.

6. He was the last man to go in the creek.

7. The track was slick.

8. She did not sit with us.

1. Fill that gold cup with milk.

2. The sheets did not fit in the truck.

3. Stick with me and we will have fun.

4. He is free to go with us.

5. She sat with Pam at the track meet.

6. That truck had a flat.

7. Will she fill this sack with seeds?

8. If it is the last meet, we will go.

[1]   [2]

1

d   n   f   l   s   n
r   m   g   w   h

2

a   i   e   o   u   ee

3

o   on   cop   sod
rock   shop   got

4

clock   tree   trap   flap
steep   drip   win   plan
seems   track   flag   truck
stop   hand   creek   sleep

5

ol   old   sold   fold   told

6

for   teeth   with   wish
ship   more   cold   sheets
store   shop   that   cash

7

said   do   was
to   have   give

8

1. The man told him, "Hop in this truck."

2. She said, "Fill this sack with fish."

3. "We do not have a clock," Jim said.

9

1. A steep hill had green grass on it.

2. If that truck can not stop, it will hit a ship.

3. Can sheep sleep on rocks?

4. His feet feel sore and cold.

5. Fold that green rag and hand it to me.

6. Will he slip in the street?

7. We plan to run the truck.

8. I can hand him the flag.

[1]

1. Pat the ram on his back.

2. Will the old man stop at the store?

3. That cold creek has rocks in it.

4. That cat sits with me in the plant.

5. Sand is still in the street.

6. He will go with the man in that truck.

7. Dad and I can pick seeds.

8. Will Pat feed the cats?

[2]

1

w h t ck r f s d n

2

e a i u ee

3

o form no nod now
go got fond cold how

4

e met fell ten neck next dent

5

(a) th sh
(b) ch wh
(c) chip when much whip
     wheel cheer chill which

6

b hub bill be rob
bed crab bad bust

7

ing sing ring bring selling
sending lifting filling meeting

8

was have to give said do of you

9

plant drop more slap fold wish

trees store chop than pole rush

greet list when blocks glass

colt torn send sore score they

10

1. She said, "How much will we spend?"

2. He said, "I keep lots of junk in that chest."

11

1. When they score, we will cheer.

2. Then I will drop it in the box next to the pole.

3. She told them, "I will see you at the meeting."

4. The man has more cats than I have.

5. Will you be selling that horse this week?

6. If you think we can do it, we will go camping.

7. How well did she do in the math class?

8. She said, "Fold up that sheet and hand it to me."

9. How much of this sand do you need?
   [1]

1. When I sing, I get a sore neck.

2. Do you think that ship will sink?

3. Set that glass on top of the shelf.

4. How much cash will they need on this trip?

5. When they get back, we will greet them with a cheer.

6. Grab this list and go to the store with it.

7. Tom was not as fast as Bill.

8. They sell chips and dip in that shop.

9. Tell me how you do that trick.
   [2]

1
w ck h t r
s d f n

2
e a u ee i

3
o form no go got
fond cold how now nod

4
e sell met end dent next lend

5
(a) th sh ch wh
(b) such whip much which
     wheel when chip chill

6
b rub rob bill bob
bed bad rust drop crab

7
ing ring thing bring filling
sanding lifting billing feeling

8
of to give said was do have you

9
drop slip more fold score
with feel sore torn chop
shop than mole rash greet
plant list colt when send
block class sore they

10

1. She said, "I wish I had a list of stores."

2. Pat said, "Bring me a glass or cup of milk."

1. They did not spend more than they had.

2. When the clocks stop, the bell will ring.

3. She is sending me to the meeting at the shop.

4. Tell them how well you ran at the track meet.

5. Hand this bag of gold to that man.

6. When we get back, I will go for a run.

7. Hold the gold, and do not drop it.

8. Do you need a lot more cash for this trip?

9. Have you seen the glass cat that was on this shelf?

[1]

1. Sell this pin to the old man at the junk shop.

2. Do you have a clock that rings?

3. She said, "How much do you like math?"

4. How can we shop if we do not have the list with us?

5. She said, "I feel a chip in my teeth."

6. I will greet them and tell them when they will sing.

7. His truck has a bad dent in the top.

8. Will the cold bring more fog?

9. The camp is at the top of this green hill.

[2]

1

o e

th wh ch sh ing

b i r d a

2

e she shell met

meet be bed

3

er her letter seller

after batter were

clerk better person

4

ing ring ringing going

doing singing sending morning

5

chops faster colt last

bets fishing sleeps

morning bring dress

were crash think sore

much cow mister

6

give was have of

said you what woman

7

1. I think we can run to the top of that hill.

2. Were you going to bring her with you?

3. The woman in the black hat sings with us.

4. Last week, we had to sell the truck.

5. She said, "Give him the rest of the milk."

6. That woman was the last person on the bus.

7. Can they get that truck to run?

8. I will ask the woman if this is her cat.

9. He said, "I did not think we had to do more math."

10. Which letter did you send her?

[1]

1. What were you doing when the bell rang?

2. They were not singing when the bus got back.

3. Have they sold that black colt yet?

4. The cow went faster than the old truck.

5. When will we win a track meet?

6. Get rid of that wet sand.

7. Bring them back to class in the morning.

8. Stop sending me sad letters.

9. After you sleep, you will feel a lot better.

10. She said, "How much did that dress cost?"

[2]

1

o   e

wh th ch ing sh

d   a   r   b   i

2

e we bell red

meet be met

3

er better clerk letter

were seller her

after batter person

4

ing sing sending morning

going doing ringing bringing

5

sleeping chips fishing

colt last bets faster

morning bring dress

cow were thank store

much cash mister

6

show blow crow snow flowing

7

have what of was

said give you woman

8

1. In the morning, they went fishing for bass.

2. Were they with you when you met her?

3. The snow was deep in the streets.

4. He said, "I think you are a better person than she is."

5. I can't drink as much milk as you can.

6. Let me show you how to fold a sheet.

7. What do you think we can do after the show?

8. Were you going to bring her letter with you?

9. She was the last person to go in that creek.

10. That old woman went for a run this morning.

[1]

1. She said, "Last week we sold the last colt."

2. Jerry and I will have fish and chips for lunch.

3. The singing was low and slow.

4. He said, "Were you in the street after the truck crash?"

5. What did the woman tell you to do?

6. "I am sending you a gift," she told her dad.

7. After his nap, he felt much better.

8. She said to the clerk, "Do you have clocks in this store?"

9. Bring me the dress with the spot on it.

10. Were you going to the store this morning?

[2]

1

o   e   ten   pond   we
teen   got   tell   wet
so   seem   get   lock

2

told   store   which   shelf   sister
over   back   path   creek   rancher
horse   going   black

3

A	B	C
plan	shop	rub
planning	shopping	rubbing
planned	shopped	rubbed

4

question   middle   said   what
you   how   down   milk
woman   do   to   person

5

Tim Asked Questions

Tim asked a lot of questions. His dad told him to go to the store for milk. Tim asked, "Which store?"

When his mom told him to set the cups on the shelf, he asked, "Which shelf?"

His sister said, "Give me a hand."

Tim said, "Which hand?"

Last week, Tim was at a ranch. The rancher told him, "Get on a horse and go down that path."

Tim asked 2 questions. What questions do you think he asked?

[1]

The rancher told Tim to get on a black horse, and Tim did that. Then Tim went down the path and got to a creek.

He said, "How is this horse going to get over this creek?"

The horse showed him how. The horse jumped over the creek. But Tim fell into the creek when the horse jumped.

Tim sat in the middle of the creek and said to the horse, "I see how you got over the creek."

Then he asked a question. What do you think he asked?

[2]

1 oo   too   broom   soon   room

2 began   before   begin

3 orders   told   pals   next   lift
were   they   sweeping   back
trash   help   set   think   just

4

A	B	C
stopping	robber	hopping
runner	sitting	robbed
grinned	dropped	stopper

5 one   where   there   gave   day
questions   what   to   do
woman   of   you   have   down
give   brown

6

Tim and His Big Sister

Tim's big sister did not ask questions. She gave orders. She told her dog what to do. She told her pals what to do. But when she told Tim what to do, he asked questions.

One day she said, "Get a broom and sweep the room."

Then Tim asked, "Which broom and which room?"

His sister said, "The red broom. Get that broom. Then sweep this room."

Tim said, "Where is the red broom?"

His sister said, "It is next to the brown broom."

Do you know what Tim asked next?

Tim's sister said, "The brown broom is in the back room."

[1]

Tim got the broom and began to sweep. Just then, his sister yelled, "Help me lift this trash can."

Tim asked, "How can I keep on sweeping and lift trash cans?"

His sister yelled, "Drop that red broom and help me."

Tim set the broom down and went to the trash can. He asked, "What is in that trash can?"

His sister got mad. She said, "What do you think is in the trash can?"

Tim said, "That is my question. If you ask questions, I will give orders."

He did just that. He told his sister what to do.

[2]

1   oo   room   soon   broom

2

A	B	C
sitting	planner	grinned
clapped	shipped	slipper
dripping	slamming	sitter

3

cold   morning   mom   socks

green   Ron's   cop   slacks

just   robbers   going   more

need   dogs   track   sister

shells   shelf   were   glad

freeze   lumps   legs

4

A	B	C
save	like	hope
saving	liking	hoping
saved	liked	hoped

5

are   my   who   have   do

one   what   before   where

there   began   day

happened   asked   filled

town   down   gave   person

Ron's Socks

On a cold morning, Ron went to his mom and said, "I have no socks."

His mom said, "You have lots and lots of socks. You have red socks for running and socks that go with black slacks."

"No, Mom," Ron said. "I do not have one sock in my room."

Ron's mom said, "If sock robbing is going on, I'll get a cop."

She did just that. The cop went in Ron's room and said, "There are no socks in this room. There must be sock robbers in this town." Then the cop said, "I will get more cops." Soon, there were 18 cops in Ron's room.

[1]

One cop said, "We need dogs to track down the sock robbers."

Just then, Ron's little sister asked, "What are cops doing in this room?" Ron told her what happened.

Ron's little sister grinned and said, "Sock robbers did not get the socks. I got the socks to hold the shells that were on my shelf."

The 18 cops were not mad. They were glad that they did not have to get dogs and track the sock robbers.

But Ron's mom was not glad. She told Ron's little sister, "Give Ron back his socks before his feet freeze."

His sister did that. Then she filled her socks with shells. Now she has big lumps on her legs.

[2]

1

kangaroo best soon hopping

sitting ever back fix

think runner bag pocket

pop were still cold

must kept more well

2

A	B
make	time
maker	timer
making	timing

3

rate rater rating

4

ice out very show

helped one there

now hopped day are

stopped before where

yelled dropped my began

Kit, the Kangaroo

5

Kit was a kangaroo. Kangaroos hop. Kit hopped as well as the best kangaroos. But one day, she stopped hopping. She said, "I can not hop." She was very sad.

A little rat was sitting next to Kit. He said, "I can help you hop."

Kit asked, "How can you do that?"

The rat said, "Let me show you how. I will be back soon. And when I get back, you will hop as well as you ever hopped before."

[1]

When the rat got back, he had a big bag. He said, "This will fix you up."

He had a big chunk of ice in the bag. He dropped the ice in Kit's pocket. As soon as he dropped the ice, Kit began to hop. She hopped up ten feet and yelled, "Get that ice out of my pock, pock, pocket."

But the ice did not pop out. She hopped up 16 feet, but the ice still did not pop out.

[1]

Kit said, "I am so cold that I can not stop hop, hop, hopping."

The rat said, "But you must keep on hopping or that ice will not pop out."

Kit kept on hopping. At last, she stopped. She said, "I can hop no more."

The rat said, "I can help you hop."

"No," Kit said. "You helped me hop before. Now I will help you." She helped that rat hop as well as a kangaroo.

How do you think she did that?

[1]

1 ea eats smear ears hear

2 fast too store much
packs must things
gum bit still
plan more chomping

3 ate rate make gave
like these here

4

A	B
hope	rider
ride	hoping
shape	later
late	shaped

5 some don't lie work oats slow
slowly show happy give one
began happened very Sandy manner
down better planning how you
there ice out are question

The Rat That Had a Fast Rate

Sandy had a rat that ate fast. She said, "That rat eats too much. I must make the rat slow down."

Sandy went to the store and got ten packs of gum. She said, "I will smear the gum on the oats." Then she gave the oats to the rat. "Here are some oats," she said. "You will have <u>fun</u> eating them."

The rat began eating at a very fast rate. But then the rate began to go down.

[1]

The rat chomped and chomped. The rat said, "I like oats, but these oats are not fun. I am chomping as fast as I can, but the oats don't go down."

Sandy said, "Ho, ho. There is gum on them so that you can not eat at a fast rate."

The rat said, "Give me the oats that do not have gum on them, and I will eat slowly."

Sandy said, "I am happy to hear that."

[1]

She gave the rat oats that did not have gum on them. The rat did 2 things. She bit Sandy's hand. Then she ate the oats at a very fast rate.

Sandy said, "You little rat. You told me a lie."

The rat said, "Yes, but did you see how fast I did it?"

Sandy said, "I will still get you to eat slowly. You will see. I have one more plan for you."

[1]

1 ea   mean   eat   beans   meat

2 fast   box   plan   too   after   help
bit   began   will   left   flash   next

3 ate   made   nose   those   these   rope

4 into   even   didn't   seven   come
hopped   oats   don't   rooms
lie   chomped   slow   slowly
show   are   dropping   slammed
some   work   days   who

5

Sandy's Plan for the Rat's Fast Rate

Sandy's rat ate at a fast rate. The rat ran at a fast rate. And it even hopped at a fast rate. Sandy had a plan to make the rat's rate go down.

Sandy got a rat that did not eat at a fast rate and did not run fast. This rat was fat. It sat and sat. When this rat ate, it chomped slowly. Sandy said, "I will take this slow rat and show my fast rat how to be slow." Sandy dropped the fat rat into the box with the fast rat.

[1]

The fast rat said, "This fat rat needs help. It is too fat. I will show it how to go fast."

Sandy's rat bit the fat rat on the nose. "Stop that," he said.

Sandy's rat said, "Make me stop."

The fat rat began to run after Sandy's rat. The rats ran and ran and ran. Then the fat rat said, "I must rest. I need to eat some oats."

Sandy's rat said, "If you don't eat fast, I will eat the oats and then no oats will be left for you."

"No," the fat rat said. "I can eat as fast as the next rat." And it did.

[1]

The fat rat was in the box with the fast rat for seven days. At the end of the seven days, the fat rat was not fat. It was fast. When Sandy dropped oats into the box, the rats ate the oats in a flash. Then the rats began to run in the box. They ran so fast that Sandy said, "I cannot see those rats. I hope they slow down."

Sandy's rat said, "This fat rat didn't make me go slow. I made his rate go up. Ho, ho."

[1]

1 oa boat float coat soap

2 went job fix smell
rest hammer hold began
bath for seating better
beef left cannot room

3 came gave make plates here

4 your other answer care
boards broken table seven
fixed some come do handed
woman grabbed asked even
into didn't slow show
work other your who

5

The Tramp at the Camp

A tramp went down a road. He came to a camp. He stopped and said, "I hate to work, but I need to eat. So I will see if I can get a job at this camp." So the tramp went to the woman who ran the camp. The tramp said, "Can I work at this camp? I can do lots of jobs."

The camp woman said, "You are a tramp."

The tramp said, "Yes, but I am a champ at camp work."

"Can you fix lamps?"

"Yes," the tramp said.

"Can you make boat ramps?"

"Yes," said the tramp. "I am the champ at ramps."

The camp woman said, "Then I will let you work in this camp." The camp woman gave the tramp a hammer. She said, "Take this hammer and make a ramp for the boats."

The tramp got boards and began to hammer. When the sun went down, he had made the boat ramp. He said, "Now I have to eat."

But the woman from the camp did not let the tramp rest. She handed the tramp a broken lamp. Then she said, "Get a clamp and fix this lamp."

So the tramp got a clamp to hold the lamp. He fixed the lamp.

[1]

[1]

The camp woman said, "Now you must take a bath. I can tell from your smell that you are not a champ at baths."

The tramp said, "No, baths are not for me."

"You will take a bath or you will not eat," the camp woman told the tramp.

The tramp ran to the eating table and grabbed ham and beef.

The tramp said, "I don't care if I smell. I can work better than the others in this camp."

A woman asked, "Do you think that you can work better than the rest of us?"

The tramp did not answer. He ate six plates of ham and seven plates of beef.

Then he said, "Now I can sleep." And he went to sleep at the table. The others left. They said, "We cannot stand the smell in here."

[2]

1   oa   roads   soaped   board   float

2   slept   felt   each   ruts   held
path   between   let's   cannot
cheered   hammered   beat
holding   bath   short   soon

3   name   woke   mile   lake
nose   came   gave   pole

4   women   because   their
pound   himself   woman
rested   seven   seventy
day   way   shows   who
your   others   answer
broken   even   very   some
come   don't   table   worker

5   # The Tramp Has a Meeting with Sam

The tramp slept at the table. The next day he woke up and felt rested. He went to the woman who ran the camp. The woman held her nose as she said, "You smell, tramp. Will you take a bath?"

"No," the tramp said.

Just then, a big man named Sam came up. He held his nose and said, "Tramp, you are not the champ worker at this camp. I am."

A woman said, "Let's have a meet between the tramp and Sam."

So the men and women set things up for the big meet. They gave a tamping pole to each man. They said, "We will see how well this tramp can tamp."

[1]

They went to the hill. The camp woman said, "Take these tamping poles and see how fast you can pound the ruts from this path."

Sam and the tramp began tamping. They tamped the path for three miles. Sam was a very fast tamper. But the tramp tamped faster. The men and women did not cheer for the tramp. They said, "That tramp can tamp fast, but Sam can make ramps faster than the tramp can."

So the tramp and Sam went to the lake. The camp woman said, "Each man will clamp seventy boards and hammer the boards on a frame. The man with the faster rate will win this meet."

[1]

Sam grabbed a clamp and began clamping boards. But the tramp clamped faster than Sam. And the tramp hammered faster than Sam.

Sam said, "I cannot work as fast as that tramp because I have to keep holding my nose when I work. I can beat him in a bath meet."

The tramp said, "No way."

The men and women cheered. They said, "Let's have a bath meet."

The camp woman handed soap to each man. The men ran to the lake with their soap. Each man soaped himself.

The tramp beat Sam. The tramp said, "That shows that I am the champ of the camp. I can clamp. I can tamp. I can even take a bath faster than you."

[2]

1

seen   champ   goat   smells
each   well   faster   just
going   shore   standing
bent   chop   kept   beat
boater   bath   cleaning   soap
beans   best   reached   cheered

2

gave   lake   nose   broke   ate

3

brother   another   paddle
other   woman   women   clapped
camping   workers   your   have
who   because   himself   their
how   down   day   say   very
slow   where   began   table

4 # The Tramp's Brother Has a Boat Meet

One day another tramp came to the camp. This tramp was big and fat. He smelled as bad as a goat. He went up to the camp woman and said, "My name is Bob. I do not like to work, but I have to eat. And I am the best worker you have seen."

The tramp who was champ of the camp went up to the camp woman and said, "That is Big Bob, my brother."

Big Bob said, "No. You can't be my brother. My brother is fat, and he smells. But you are not fat, and you do not smell."

The tramp said, "But I am your brother."

The camp woman said, "We do not need more workers in this camp."

The tramp said, "But you need boaters. And Big Bob is the best there is."

The camp woman held her nose. She said, "We will see how well Big Bob can do in a boat meet with Sam."

[1]

Each man got in a boat. But Big Bob had an old boat that was very slow.

[1]

The camp woman said, "When I clap, begin paddling. Paddle as fast as you can to the other shore of the lake."

The camp woman clapped and the men began to paddle. Soon Big Bob's boat was next to Sam's boat. Just then, Bob's paddle broke and Bob's boat began to slow down. Sam's boat kept on going. The camp woman was standing on the shore. She said, "Big Bob cannot beat Sam now."

Bob bent down and began to paddle with his hands. His hands went chop, chop, chop into the lake. And his old boat began to go faster and faster.

[1]

Before Sam reached the other shore, Big Bob went past him. Men and women cheered. Even the camp woman said, "Bob is the best boater I have seen."

Then the others said, "Let's get brother Bob to take a bath." They held their noses and ran to Big Bob. They went in the lake with him and began cleaning him with soap. When Big Bob left the lake, he did not smell.

The men and women said, "Now, let's go to the eating table." So the tramp and his brother and the other workers went to the eating table, where they ate and ate.

[1]

1

shed lock fix horn

pen his pick tock

fell bang reached

keep bop seen

ever broom hear

2

A	B
pole	later
broke	likes
late	poles
note	liking
came	broken
like	notes

3

door someone handle from

are work even now

brother very every show

grabbed who paddle locked

clocked these those hammers

tamping bother another

The Clock Maker at the Camp

The tramp and his brother Big Bob went to the shed. The tramp grabbed the handle of the door. He said, "This door has a lock on it. How will we get in the shed? The hammers and the tamping poles are in the shed. We need hammers and tampers if we are to work."

Big Bob said, "Brother, don't bother with that lock. I will kick the door in."

"No," the tramp said. "Let's go to the camp woman and see if she can get in this shed."

So they went to the camp woman. The camp woman said, "I will get a man to fix that lock."

[1]

Later, an old man came to the camp. He had a big bag and a big horn that he held to his ear.

He said, "I am here to fix the clock."

The men said, "We do not need someone to fix a clock. We need someone to fix a lock. We cannot get in the shed. The door is locked."

The old man said, "You say the door is clocked?"

Big Bob said, "Make a note for the old man. Even with his ear horn, he cannot hear."

So the tramp got a pen and made a note. The note said, "We need to get in the shed, but the shed is locked."

The old man said, "I cannot help you. I work on clocks, not locks."

[2]

So Big Bob got a pick and began to pick the lock. The lock began to go, "Tick, tick, tock, tock."

The tramp said, "This lock is ticking like a clock."

The old man grabbed a hammer from his bag and hit the lock with the hammer. The lock fell from the door. The lock went, "Bing, bang, bop."

The men went into the shed and got their tamping poles and their hammers. Then they went to work. The old man picked up the broken lock and said, "I will keep this clock. It is the best clock I have seen."

[1]

1

con road lid mop

near shore faster loading

slop must eating prop

glad each left moon

clean crack tore bits

begin mess sold

2

came take like slope

these those hate

3

dropped fatter grabbed mopped

slopping conned mopping

4

dollars seventeen how because

other handle door from

someone yelled ever every

give handed works what

workers brother another

5   The Tramp Meets the Con Man

A con man came to the camp. That con man came up the camp road with a box. The camp woman met him.

The con man dropped his box and held the lid up. He grabbed a mop from the box. He said, "The workers will like this mop. It is fatter than other mops. So a worker can mop faster with this mop."

The camp woman said, "I will get someone to take that mop and see how well it works." So the camp woman yelled for the tramp.

[1]

The tramp was on a slope near a shore of the lake. Was he making a ramp? No, he was raking slop near the pond. He was a fast slop raker. He went to the con man and the camp woman. The camp woman handed the mop to the tramp.

"Here," she said. "See if this fatter mop mops faster than other mops."

The tramp said, "I hate to stop slopping to do some mopping."

The camp woman said, "When I say that you must mop, you must mop. So take this fat mop and begin mopping."

[1]

But the tramp did not begin mopping. He went to the eating table and said, "I will prop this mop near the door, and I will sit. Then I will go back and tell the others that I mopped." So that is what the tramp did.

After he sat, he went back to the camp woman and the con man. He said, "Yes, this fat mop is the best mop I have ever seen."

The camp woman told the con man, "We will take seventeen of those fatter mops."

The con man was glad to sell the mops. He handed seventeen mops to the camp woman and told the camp woman, "Give me 50 dollars."

[1]

When the con man left, the camp woman yelled for the workers. She handed each woman and man a mop. Then she said, "Take the mops and clean every crack in this camp."

The workers began to mop. But the mops did not work. When they got wet, they tore into little bits. A woman said, "These mops make a mess."

That con man had sold the camp woman bad mops. He had conned her. He got 50 dollars from the camp woman. She had seventeen mop handles and a big mess.

[1]

1

dress   near   road   lead
shed   stream   chips   shack
order   bench   gloom   coat
basket   deal   thank   that's
free   grass   lunch

2

late   slope   these   those   five

3

cook   folks   throw   I've   can't
one   of   dollars   seventeen   who
day   play   didn't   worked   packer
what   matter   where   dressed
lifted   show   begin   because   between

Cathy and a Band at the Bend

4

Cathy worked in a dress shop. One day she said, "I need a rest." So she went to her pal, Pam. She said, "Pam, let us go to hear a band play. A band is near the bend in the road. They play well."

Then Cathy and Pam went to hear the band. When they got near the bend in the road, Pam said, "I need to eat. Let me lead you to a little shed. It is near the stream. They sell fish and chips in that shed."

[1]

So Pam led Cathy to the fish shed near the stream. The shack was packed with folks. The folks were yelling, "I was next. Give me my order of fish and chips."

Pam said, "This is a mess."

Cathy and Pam left the fish shed and sat on a bench. A man came up to them. He had a net, and he was dressed in a big coat. He set the net in the sand, and then he sat down on the bench. He asked Cathy, "What is the matter?"

Cathy said, "The shed is packed. We will be late to hear the band."

[1]

The man said, "I am a fish packer. If you need fish, let me help you."

The man went to his boat in the stream. Then he came back with a basket. Cathy said, "Let me pay you for those fish."

"Give me five dollars," the man said.

"That is a deal," Cathy said. "Thank you." She said to Pam, "I've got lots of fish."

Pam said, "But they are not cooked."

"I didn't think of that," Cathy said.

Then Cathy grabbed the basket of fish and ran into the fish shed.

[1]

"What are you going to do?" Pam asked.

Cathy said to the man in the fish shed, "Cook these fish and you can keep five of them."

"That's a deal," the man said.

After the man fixed the fish, Pam said, "Can you throw in some free chips?" The man did that.

Then Cathy and Pam left the shed near the stream. When they got to the band at the bend in the road, they set their basket of fish in the grass. Then they sat on a bench to hear the band and eat their lunch.

[1]

1

cold   store   that   read   back
soon   job   beans   helped
ham   better   things   much

2

name   like   came   note   bone   home

3

Gretta   Chee   let's   day   pay   played
stay   someone   saying   door   bigger   said
I've   cook   other   some   don't   can't
folks   didn't   another   their   became   one

4

Chee, the Dog

Gretta got a little dog. She named the dog Chee. Chee got bigger and bigger each day.

On a very cold day, Gretta said, "Chee, I must go to the store. You stay home. I will be back."

Chee said, "Store, lots, of, for, no."

Then Gretta said, "Did I hear that dog say things?"

Chee said, "Say things can I do."

Gretta said, "Dogs don't say things. So I must not hear things well."

But Chee did say things. Gretta left the dog at home. When Gretta came back, Chee was sitting near the door.

[1]

Gretta said, "That dog is bigger than she was."

Then the dog said, "Read, read for me of left."

Gretta said, "Is that dog saying that she can read?" Gretta got a pad and made a note for the dog. The note said, "Dear Chee, if you can read this note, I will hand you a bag of bones."

Gretta said, "Let's see if you can read."

Chee said, "Dear Chee, if you can read this note, I will ham you a bag for beans."

[1]

Gretta said, "She can read, but she can't read well. Ho, ho."

Chee became very mad. She said, "For note don't read ho ho."

Gretta said, "Chee gets mad when I say ho, ho."

Chee said, "Yes, no go ho ho."

Then Gretta felt sad. She said, "I didn't mean to make you mad. I don't like you to be sad. I will help you say things well."

Then Chee said, "Yes, well, of say for things."

So every day, Gretta helped Chee say things. She helped Chee read, too.

[1]

Chee got better and better at saying things. And she got better at reading. And she got bigger and bigger. When she was one year old, she was bigger than Gretta.

On a hot day Gretta left Chee at home, but when she got back, Chee met her at the door. "Did you have fun at your job?" Chee asked.

"Yes, I did," Gretta said.

"I don't have much fun at home," Chee said. "I think I will get a job. I don't like to stay at home."

"Dogs can't have jobs," Gretta said.

Chee said, "You have a job. So I will get a job, too."

[1]

1

clock   hear   locked   near
conning   pack   road   met
corn   shed   sled   told
sack   deal   horn   room

2

A	B
make	trades
like	maker
trade	saving
save	liked
	traded

3

ready   folks   from   show   grow
grower   dressed   don't   yelled
grabbed   dropped   handed   I've
some   day   cook   stamped

4

shade   here   made   like   trade

5

The Old Clock Maker and the Con Man

The old clock maker did not hear well. He left the camp with the lock. He had the lock in his pack. He went down the road from the camp. Then he met a corn grower.

But the corn grower was not a corn grower. He was the con man dressed up like a corn grower. The con man liked conning folks.

The con man said, "Let's go sit in the shade near my shed."

"Yes," the clock maker said, "I will trade for a bed."

"No, not a bed," the con man said. "Shed. We will sit near the shed."

The clock maker said, "Yes, I like a sled, but I don't see a sled."

[1]

The con man was mad at the clock maker. He yelled, "WE WILL SIT IN THE SHADE."

"Yes," the clock maker said. "I am ready to trade."

The con man led the clock maker to the shade. He held the clock maker's horn to the clock maker's ear. Then he said, "Will you trade your pack for some corn?"

"No," the clock maker said, "I need this horn. So I will not trade this horn. But I will trade my pack for corn."

The con man got a sack of corn. He set the sack near the shed.

Then the con man went into the shed and got a very big horn. He said, "Hold this horn to your ear and you will hear me better."

[2]

The clock maker said, "Yes, that deal seems better. I will trade my little horn for this big horn."

The clock maker grabbed the big horn and dropped it into his pack. He handed his little horn to the con man. "Here," he said. "Now this is your horn. We have traded horns."

"No, no," the con man yelled.

The clock maker said, "Yes, I have made my trade for the day. Now I must go." So he did.

The con man was very mad. He stamped up and down. Then he asked, "How did that man con me out of my horn? He has the big horn, and I just have a little horn and some corn."

[1]

1
tears   fun   cheeks   brick   plant
molds   speak   load   leave   still   hearing

2
felt   self   left   get   went   help

3
bake   here   fire   home

4
boss   herself   station
something   question   can't
saying   from   fireman   didn't
patted   over   himself   began
ready   Chee   Gretta   upset

5
Chee Goes for a Job

Chee felt sad. So she left her home to get a job.

Chee went to a fire station. She went up to the man who ran the station and said, "I need a job. Can you help me?"

The man said, "Is my hearing going bad or did that dog say something to me?"

The dog said, "I did say something. Do you have a job for me?"

The man said, "Ho, ho. That dog is saying things, but dogs can't speak."

[1]

Chee got so mad that she began to say odd things. "Fire station for of to go," she said.

The man said, "Ho, ho. This dog is fun. I will keep this dog with me. I like to hear the odd things that dog can say."

Chee was so mad at the fireman she said, "From of for, fireman."

The fireman fell down and went, "Ho, ho, ho." He had tears on his cheeks. His ears got red. Then he patted Chee and said, "I didn't mean to make you mad. But you do say odd things."

[1]

Then the dog said to herself, "I will not work here. I can't stand to hear that fireman go, 'Ho, ho.' "

So Chee left the station. She went down the road to a brick plant. The man in the brick plant said, "Well, well, I see a dog in this plant."

"Yes," Chee said. Then she asked the man, "Can I have a job here?"

The man said, "What have we here? A dog that can say things." Then he asked, "Can you help bake bricks?"

"I think so," Chee said.

[1]

The man asked, "Can you fill brick molds?"

"Yes," Chee said.

Then the man said, "But you are a dog. I do not think that I can hire you." The man began to think. At last he said, "I will get my boss. He will tell me what to do."

The man left and came back with his boss. The boss said to Chee, "I will hire you if you can lift that load of bricks."

But she did not lift the bricks. She got upset and said, "Much bricks lift, no." She showed her teeth.

The boss said, "Leave this plant."

So Chee left. She still did not have a job.

[1]

1

ranch faster chopped
goats checked horses
bent slap leave heels
loafers swam swim jab

2

rode named rider safe
makes side tame time

3

Emma anyone nobody good
because let's boss didn't
ready their Flop woman
women milked herself station
question biggest stayed Branch

4

The Rancher

There was a big ranch in the West. The rancher who ran this ranch was named Emma Branch. She rode a horse well. She chopped fast, and she swam faster. The men and women who worked for Emma Branch liked her. They said, "She is the best in the West." On her ranch she had sheep and she had cows. There were goats and horses. There was a lot <u>of</u> grass.

The rancher had a lot of women and men working for her. They worked with the sheep and the goats, and they milked the cows. Each worker had a horse. But the rancher's horse was the biggest and the best. It was a big, black horse named Flop.

[1]

Flop got its name because it reared up. When Flop reared up, any rider on it fell down and went "flop" in the grass. But Flop did not rear up when the rancher rode it. Emma Branch bent near Flop's ear and said, "Let's go, Flop." And they went. She did not have to slap the horse. She didn't have to jab her heels and yell at Flop. She just said, "Let's go," and they went like a shot.

Every day, she checked up on the workers to see what they were doing. She checked to see that they were working well and that they were not loafing.

[1]

If a worker was loafing, Emma told the worker, "I will say this for the last time: 'Do not loaf on this ranch any more.' " If a worker was loafing the next time she checked, she said, "Go from my ranch. We do not need loafers here."

The women and men who worked on the ranch said, "When you hear Flop running, you had better be working. If you are not working, you had better get ready to leave this ranch."

But the workers that stayed at the ranch liked to work for Emma Branch. They said, "We like to have Emma on our side. We can see how mean Flop is, and he is very tame when Emma rides him. So it's good to have Emma on your side."

[2]

1

plant   tears   stacks   kept   sore
Chee   cheeks   easy   just   slab

2

A	B	C
slow	slowest	slowly
near	nearly	nearest
safe	safest	safely
fast	faster	fastest

3

slate   came   pile   rate   side

4

money   you'll   look   good
things   sense   clapped   may
saying   showed   hands   way
think   picked   that's   odd
worked   cannot   began   ever
because   added   stackers
never   anyone   nobody

5

Chee Stacks Slate

Chee went to get a job, but no plant had jobs for dogs that say things. At last, Chee went to a slate plant. Chee said, "I hope that I can get a job here." Chee went into the plant. Chee went past stacks of slate. She came to the woman who ran the plant. Chee asked, "Do you have a job I can do in this plant?"

The woman looked at Chee. Then the woman said, "Ho, ho, ho. I cannot help going 'Ho, ho, ho.'"

Chee got so mad that she began to say odd things. "Stop slate for from me, of go so no to do, ho ho."

The woman fell down and kept going, "Ho, ho, ho."

Chee felt so mad that she did not stop saying odd things.

The woman got sore from going "ho, ho." She had lots of tears on her cheeks. Then she stopped ho-hoing and said, "I have seen lots of

[1]

things, but I have never seen a dog that said odd things."

[1]

Chee was not so mad now. So Chee began to say things that made sense. Chee said, "I told you not to go 'ho, ho.' I told you that I need a job."

The woman got up and clapped her hands. She said, "Let me see. I think I may have a job for you." The woman's cheeks still had tears on them. She asked, "Can you stack slate?"

Chee said, "I think so."

The woman showed Chee how to stack slate.

[1]

The woman said, "Stacking is easy. You just pick up a slab of slate and set it on top of your pile." Chee picked up a slab and set it on the pile.

"That's the way to do it," the woman said. Then she added, "See how fast you can stack. The faster you stack, the more money you'll make."

So Chee began her job as a slate stacker. Each day, her rate went up. She worked at the plant for nearly a year. At the end of the year, she was one of the fastest stackers in the plant.

[1]

1
shearing   helper   than   locks
pants   sheets   planned   holding
steal   still   chest   every

2
hope   rate   shaved   nose   fake   those

3

A	B	C
shape	shaping	shapely
like	likely	liked
cold	coldest	colder
short	shortly	shortest

4
wool   look   good   even
stay   show   felt   ready
someone   where   there
money   before   grabbed

5

The Con Man and the Sheep Rancher

Emma Branch had a lot of big sheep on her ranch. One day she said, "My sheep need shearing. I will send for a sheep shearer."

So she told one of her helpers to go to town and get someone who can shear sheep. The helper went down the road to town. But he did not get there. He met the con man on the road. The con man said, "Where are you going?"

The helper said, "The rancher needs her sheep sheared."

The con man said, "I am the best at shearing sheep. I have shears in my pack."

So Emma's helper led the con man back to the ranch. When they got there, Emma yelled from the door, "I hope that man can shear fast."

[1]

The con man said, "I can shave sheep. I can shape. And I can shear."

"But how is your rate at shearing?" the rancher asked.

"I can go so fast that I can shave a sheep before it sees the shears. You can shop and shop, but you cannot get someone who can shape or shave faster than me."

So the con man got the job. He told the rancher to get him ten sacks for holding the wool.

The con man had a plan. He did not plan to shear sheep. He planned to steal sheep. He planned to pack sheep into sacks. Then he planned to take those sacks and run from the ranch.

[1]

But his plan did not work very well. The rancher did not leave him. She said, "I will stay and see how fast you shear."

The con man had never sheared sheep before. He got the shears from his pack and grabbed a sheep. The sheep ran from the con man. The rancher said, "Ho, ho. You can't even hold a sheep. Let me show you how." The rancher grabbed a sheep and sat on its nose. Then she said, "Now I've got this sheep. You shave it."

The con man began to shave that sheep, but the sheep did not stay still.

[1]

The con man shaved the rancher's leg. Then the con man shaved the hay near the sheep. Then the con man shaved his hand.

"Ho, ho," the rancher said. "You are a fake. You cannot shave sheep. You have never held shears before. Let me show you how to do that job."

She grabbed the con man and held him down. She sat on his back and began to shave him. She shaved his locks. She shaved his coat. She shaved his pants. She shaved his legs. She even shaved his chest. When he was shaved, she said, "Now you see how to shave. Pack up your shears and leave this ranch."

When the con man left the ranch, he felt very cold.

[2]

1

nearly slop more year

bum rest bath morning

stack flash weeks deal

2

lake raked shade time

rider take shaved fake

3

person believe any beans

town stay show seven

happened hammers boards

look women wool can't

where conning workers

4

The Rancher and the Tramp

The tramp had worked at the camp for nearly a year. He had tamped and made ramps. He had fixed lamps and raked slop near the lake. But now he said, "I think I will leave this camp. I am a tramp, and tramps don't stay in a camp for more than a year."

So the tramp got his pack and went to the camp woman. He told her, "I must go now. The work here is getting old, and I need a rest. I will go sit in the shade and eat beans and rest. It is time to go where I do not have to take a bath."

So the tramp left and went down the camp road. When he got to a town, he said, "I see a person on a big, black horse. I will ask that rider where I can go to rest in the shade." The tramp went up to the person on the black horse and said, "Tell me, where can I go to rest in the shade?"

The person on the horse was Emma Branch. She was the rancher that shaved the con man. She said, "You are a tramp, and I do not help tramps. I help men and women who work well."

[1]

"I work well," the tramp said. "But I am sick of working. I need a rest."

[1]

The rancher said to the tramp, "I can tell that you do not like to work. You are a tramp."

That made the tramp mad. He said, "Yes, I am a tramp. But I like to work. And I can work better than any of the workers on your ranch. I work faster than any ranch hand you have ever seen."

"Ho, ho," the rancher said. "The last man who said he was a fast worker did not do a thing. He was a fake. And I think you are a fake, too."

The tramp got so mad that he got a hammer from his sack. He went to a stack of boards. In a flash, the tramp made a little shed from the boards.

[1]

The rancher did not believe what happened. Then she said, "That was the fastest hammering I have ever seen. But how are you at shearing sheep?"

"I can shear faster than I can hammer," the tramp said.

The rancher said, "If you show me that you can shear sheep that fast, I will let you sit in the shade on my ranch for seven weeks. But if you are conning me, I will hold you down and shave you."

The tramp said, "It is a deal."

So the rancher and the tramp went to the ranch. The rancher said, "When the sun comes up in the morning, we will see how well you shear."

[2]

1 near felt morning heaps
flashed sweeping reached
shears melt jerk plop

2 wake nose shaving five

3 minutes handed rested may
wool cannot work have any
grabbed wow out seven
slow sleeping look took
good cook very down
don't believe person yelled

4 The Tramp Shows the Rancher How to Shear

The sun came up in the morning. The tramp was sleeping near a big sheep shed. The rancher's helper came to wake him up.

The tramp said, "Leave me be. I am sleeping." So the tramp went back to sleep.

The helper ran to Emma and said, "That tramp didn't get up when I went to wake him up."

Emma grabbed shears and ran over to the tramp. The helper ran with her. When they got to the tramp, the rancher handed the shears to her helper. She said to the tramp, "If you don't get up, my helper will give you a shearing."

So the tramp got up and went to the sheep shed with Emma.

[1]

Emma said, "We have a deal. If you can shear 50 sheep as fast as you hammer, you may stay and rest on my ranch."

Then she handed the shears to the tramp. The tramp felt more like sleeping than shearing. He said, "I did not sleep well. When I am not rested, I cannot work well. I will have to jump up and down to wake up." So the tramp began to jump up and down. Then the tramp said, "Now I can shear sheep."

"Good," Emma said. "You have 50 minutes to shear 50 sheep." Like a flash the tramp went for a sheep.

[1]

He grabbed the sheep and sat on its nose. The shears flashed in the sun. And wool went plop, plop from the sheep. The rancher said, "Wow! That's fast shearing. This tramp has made heaps and heaps of wool."

The tramp was shearing sheep faster than the helper was sweeping up the wool. "Slow down," the helper yelled. "I cannot sweep that fast."

The tramp said, "Don't tell me to slow down, or I will take these shears and give you a shaving."

In less than five minutes, the 50 sheep had been sheared. The tramp handed the shears to the rancher. "Here," he said. "I have sheared those sheep."

The rancher dropped the shears. "They are hot," she said.

[1]

The tramp said, "When I shear sheep, I go so fast that the shears may melt."

The rancher asked, "Where is my helper? I do not see him."

"Is he in that heap of wool?" the tramp asked.

"Yes, yes," the helper said. "I am in this heap and I cannot see a thing."

The tramp reached into the heap and grabbed the helper's hand. He gave the hand a jerk. And out came the helper. The rancher said, "That tramp can shear sheep faster than you can sweep wool."

So Emma kept her deal with the tramp. The tramp rested on her ranch for seven weeks. And every day, the helper took big meals to the tramp. Each day, the tramp rested and ate.

[2]

LESSON **31**

1

meals   between   until
horse   plan   win
better   bets   shearing

2

A	B	C
neat	neatly	neatest
broke	broken	broker
year	yearly	years
beat	beater	beaten

3

ate   lake   shade   shaved
shame   like   shape

4

Shelly   people   stayed   wool
bragged   anyone   town   dollars
other   slower   have   look
things   handed   hated   rested
week   don't   didn't   let's

5 The Rancher Sets Up a Shearing Meet

The tramp had stayed at the ranch for seven weeks. Every day, he had big meals of beef and ham and beans and corn. Every day, he sat in the shade near the lake. And every day, he got a little slower. He got slower and slower with each meal that he ate.

The rancher did not think that the tramp was slow. She had seen him go so fast that the helper did not sweep the wool as fast as the tramp shaved sheep.

Emma went to town and bragged. She said, "There is a tramp on my ranch that can shear sheep faster than anyone you have seen."

[1]

When Emma was in town one day, she told a lot of people, "My tramp can beat anyone in a shearing meet."

A woman named Shelly stepped up to Emma and said, "I think I can beat anyone in a shearing meet."

"Let's have a meet," the others yelled.

"Yes," the rancher said.

So they set up a meet between the tramp and Shelly. A man said, "Let's make bets. I will bet on Shelly. I have seen her work with shears, and I think she can beat any old tramp."

The rancher said, "I will bet ten dollars on my tramp." Then she made other bets.

[1]

When Emma got back to the ranch, she told the tramp, "Your seven weeks are up. If you stay, you will have to work."

"That is a shame," he said. "I hate to work. So I will have to leave."

The rancher said, "I will make a deal with you. We will have a shearing meet between you and Shelly. If you win that meet, you may stay here on the ranch. And you will not have to work every day. I will make you do a little work now and then. But if you do not win the meet, you will have to work like a horse."

The tramp said, "Yes, I like that plan."

[2]

The rancher said, "We will have the meet at the end of this week. So get in shape."

"Yes, yes," the fat tramp said.

"I mean it," the rancher said. "You seem to be in bad shape. You have rested for seven weeks. Now you don't look like you can do things very fast."

The tramp said, "Well, I am the best, and I will win that shearing meet. But I will need a lot of rest until the day of the meet."

"I hope you can shear better than you look," Emma said.

"Yes, yes," the tramp said. And then he went back to sleep.

[1]

1

told corn faster sheared

cheered pick beaten flash

west heap sore speed

2

shape shaved hope

pile fake shamed

3

all slower turn anyone

down town before wool into

landed rested melted others

yelled Shelly every begin

working now dropping show

The Shearing Meet

The rancher had told the tramp to get in shape for the shearing meet. But did the tramp get in shape? No. He ate big meals of corn and ham and beans and meat. Then he went to sleep.

Was the tramp in shape at the end of the week? No. The tramp was out of shape and very slow.

The people from town came to the ranch with Shelly. Shelly was in tip-top shape. Before the meet began, she sheared a sheep to show the others how fast she was. Before the wool that fell from the sheep landed, the sheep was shaved from one end to the other.

[1]

The people cheered. "Shelly can beat anyone at shearing," they yelled.

The tramp had to work to pick up the shears. He said, "I may have rested too much, but when I get going, I will speed up."

The rancher said, "Shelly and the tramp will shear all day."

The tramp said to his helper, "I hope you are fast at sweeping. The wool will be dropping very fast."

The rancher said, "Go," and the shearing began.

[1]

The tramp's shears did not go like a flash. And the wool did not pile up fast. "I must go faster," he said. But he did not go faster. He went slower. He ran the shears into the sheep's ear, and the sheep bit him on the leg. Then the sheep got up and ran from the shed.

The people said, "Ho, ho. That tramp can't shear. But Shelly is going like a shot."

Shelly had sheared three sheep and she was working on the next sheep. Her helper was up to his ears in wool. "I need help," the helper yelled.

[1]

The tramp's helper said, "I can help you now. This tramp is so slow that he will never make a pile of wool."

So the tramp's helper began to help Shelly's helper. And the tramp went to get the sheep that ran from him. When he got the sheep, Shelly had shaved seven sheep.

They sheared for the rest of the day. When the sun was going down in the west, Shelly had sheared 500 sheep. The tramp had sheared 4 sheep. Shelly had melted three shears. The tramp's shears were cold.

[1]

Shelly had made a heap of wool as big as a hill. The tramp had made a pile of wool as big as a little sheep.

Emma was yelling at the tramp. "You are a fake."

The rancher said to the others, "My tramp did not win this meet, so I will pay you for the bets that I made."

When the other people left, the rancher went to the tramp. She said, "In the morning, you are going to begin work. And you will work like a horse every day."

The tramp felt bad. He did not say a thing. He was sore. He was shamed. He had never been beaten in a meet before.

[1]

1 peeking picked more dug sore
hammer east beginning lend next

---

2 ate gate holes shape
gave shaving five

---

3 you're worked egg handed
may very every even all
there another dollars people
seventy others odds one
any meal beaten broken
ready three boards planted

The Tramp Gets in Shape

The tramp worked and worked at the ranch. Every day, he got up when the sun was peeking over the hill in the east. The tramp did not eat a big meal. He went to the sheep shed and sheared sheep. Then he picked corn. Then he ate a little meal. He had an egg and a little bit of ham. He said, "I need more to eat."

"No more," the rancher said. "Back to work for you." She handed the tramp a hammer. "Take boards and make a gate," she said.

[1]

After the tramp had made a gate, the rancher said, "Now take boards and make a pen for goats." After the tramp had made a pen of boards, she said, "Next, you're going to dig holes for planting trees."

So the tramp dug tree holes. Then he planted trees. Then he sheared more sheep. At last, the rancher said, "Now you may eat a meal."

But it was a very little meal. The tramp ate it and said, "I need more to eat."

"No more," she said. And she gave the tramp more work.

[1]

At the end of the day, the tramp was sore. He was sore the next day.

But at the end of the week, he began to get faster. His hammer began to go like a flash. His shears began to get hot when he was shaving sheep. The tramp was beginning to get back in shape.

The tramp worked for five weeks. And he got a little faster every week. He had worked so fast that there was no more work at the ranch. So he went to the rancher and said, "Send your helper to town and tell Shelly that I am ready for another shearing meet."

[1]

The rancher said, "I will send my helper to town. But I will not make bets on you."

The tramp said, "I will bet on me. Lend me seventy dollars."

So the rancher lent seventy dollars to the tramp. Then she sent her helper to town. The helper told the people, "The tramp says he can beat Shelly in a shearing meet."

The others said, "Ho, ho."

The helper told them, "But the tramp will bet that he can beat Shelly. He has seventy dollars and he will bet if he gets odds."

[1]

Shelly said, "That tramp is so bad at shearing that he needs very big odds. I will bet at three to one odds."

"So will I," the others said.

So the helper bet the tramp's seventy dollars at 3 to 1 odds. He said, "This means that the tramp will get 210 dollars if he beats Shelly in the meet."

The others said, "But we don't think there is any way he can beat Shelly."

The helper went back to the ranch and told the tramp that he had made bets at three to one odds.

"I like those odds," the tramp said. "I will win this next meet."

[1]

1 ai

A	B
wait	waited
paint	pain
sail	grain
main	fail

2 beaten   road   cheered
real   keep   before

3 gates   shape   waved   here's
saving   shaved   five   broken

4 planted   worked   faster   people
yelled   town   didn't   grabbed
seventeen   all   wool   slow
begged   planned   let's   you're
panting   handed   speed   ready

5

The Meet with Shelly Is Set

The tramp felt he was in shape for the shearing meet. When there was no more work on Emma's ranch, the tramp did some work at the next ranch, so he could stay in shape. He made ten gates. He planted 600 trees. He sheared 950 sheep. The helpers that worked on this ranch said, "He is the fastest worker in the land."

Shelly did not get in shape. She said, "I am in shape. My hands are fast. I have never been beaten in a shearing meet."

On the day of the meet, the tramp sat near the ranch gate. The people from town came up the road. They waved to the tramp.

[1]

The people said, "We made bets that Shelly will beat you." Then they went to the sheep shed and waited.

When Shelly came up the road, the people cheered. "Here's Shelly," they yelled.

Just before the meet began, Emma Branch came up to the tramp. She said, "If you do not beat Shelly, I will not let you stay here. You will have to get your things and leave this ranch."

The tramp didn't say a thing. He just sat and waited.

"We are ready for a shearing meet," a woman yelled. "Let's go."

[1]

The tramp ran fast as a shot. He grabbed his shears and said, "I will need three helpers. I will make heaps of wool so fast that 2 helpers will not keep up with me."

The others said, "Ho, ho." Seven people said, "We will help with wool if you need us." Then they said, "Ho, ho."

Shelly and the tramp held their shears and waited. Then the rancher said, "Go," and they began shearing. The tramp went so fast that he had sheared 2 sheep before Shelly ran her shears over one sheep. When Shelly had sheared seven sheep, the tramp had sheared 46 sheep.

[1]

The tramp made heaps of wool so fast that his helpers yelled, "Help!"

So the seven people who had said, "We will help," began to bag heaps of wool. But the tramp went so fast that they did not keep up with him. They begged, "Slow down. We cannot bag wool this fast."

"No," the tramp said. "I will not slow down. I have been saving my real speed for the end of this meet. And here I go." The tramp had shaved 4 sheep as he told them what he planned to do. Now he went so fast that seven more people had to help bag wool.

[1]

At the end of the meet, the tramp had sheared 9000 sheep. Shelly had sheared 501 sheep. Seventeen people were panting. They said, "We made a bad bet. Now we have to pay three to one odds to that tramp." So they did.

Then the tramp handed his 210 dollars to the rancher and said, "Now we are even. You bet on me before and I was beaten. So take this 210 dollars."

"No," Emma said. "Pay me the seventy dollars I lent you. That will make us even." Then the rancher said, "You see, I made a bet on this meet, too. You worked so fast this week that I bet 100 dollars at five to one odds."

[1]

1 ai

A	B
rain	fail
grain	sailed
waited	main

2 stacker nearly luck sleeves shabby
coats room runs seated desk

3 quit yellow button else
Rop box people showed
slowly who another slam
all stepped sloppy slid
any ready one sobbed
something seventy stamped
person grabbed slapped

4

Chee Meets Rop

Chee worked as a slate stacker for nearly a year. By then, her rate of stacking was very good. But she was getting a little sick of her job. "Stack, stack, stack," she said. "It's time to do something else." So she went to the woman who ran the slate plant and said, "I think I have to quit and get another job."

The woman said, "You have been a good worker. Good luck."

Chee left the plant and went looking for work. She came to a sleeve plant. They made sleeves for coats in this plant.

Chee went into the plant and said to the people working in a big room, "Where is the person who runs this plant?"

They went, "Ho, ho. We do not work for a person."

Chee told them, "You must work for someone. Show me who."

A man stepped up to Chee. The man said, "Step into that room and you will see who runs this plant. His name is Rop."

[1]

So Chee stepped into the room. Then she stopped. There was no man seated at the desk. There was a yellow dog at the desk.

[1]

The yellow dog slapped a stamp on a letter. Then he pressed a button. A man came into the room. The yellow dog said, "I have stamped this letter. Get it into the mail box now."

The man grabbed the letter and ran from the room. "Don't slam the door," the yellow dog yelled.

The man did not slam the door. When the man had left the room, the yellow dog slowly got up from the desk. He said to Chee, "Leave this room. Pets cannot stay here. I told the people who work for me they cannot have pets here. So go home, you shabby dog."

[1]

"Shabby dog?" Chee said. "I am not a shabby dog, you sloppy yellow dog. I am not a pet. I can do more things than you can."

The yellow dog showed his teeth. Then he said, "I run this plant. You are just a dog.

Seventy people work for me. No one works for you. I make a lot of dollars each week. I'll bet that you don't have one dollar. And you don't say things very well."

Chee showed her teeth. She was so mad that she began to say odd things.

[1]

Chee said, "Slob, slab, you speak well, for more of people beat I bet, you yellow shabby."

The yellow dog was ho-hoing like mad. He fell down and sobbed, "Ho, ho." Tears slid from his nose. His nose got red.

Chee said, "Stop, you slob ho-hoing, I let for slapping of your shabby yellow, you bum."

Then Rop stopped ho-hoing. He said, "If you think you are better than me, we will have a meet. I will show you that I can beat you in any meet you name."

Chee said, "With or of OK."

[1]

1

sleeving fresh store slabs score
checkers slap chomp gromp

2

named scale same sale jokes

3

fantastic I'll yellow doing between
yelled going ready next other one
questions played quit sense else
slop button silly stammer yet

4

Rop and Chee Have a Meet

Chee had met a yellow dog in a sleeve plant. The yellow dog was named Rop, and he ran the plant. He said that he was better than Chee at doing things. Chee got mad. So a meet was set between Rop and Chee. Rop said, "We will see if you can beat me in this meet."

Rop yelled to the workers in the sleeve plant. "Stop sleeving and get in here fast," he said. The workers ran into the room. Rop said, "Chee and I are going to have a meet. We will begin by seeing how fast we can eat."

[1]

Rop told a worker, "Get me 2 slabs of fresh meat. Drop the slabs on the scale and see that they are the same."

A woman ran from the plant. She went to the store. She grabbed 2 slabs of meat that were on sale. She got back to the plant and dropped them on the scale. Each slab was the same.

Rop handed a slab to Chee. "Here's your slab. See if you can keep up with me." Then he said, "When you hear me say, 'Go,' get your teeth into that meat. Get set . . ."

[1]

Chee was ready to eat. She was not going to let that yellow dog beat her at eating meat.

"Go," Rop said. And Chee went. Chomp, chomp, gromp, clop.

But Chee did not beat Rop, and Rop did not beat Chee. Their score was the same. Rop was mad. He said, "I did not beat her at eating, but I will get the best score in the next thing we do. We will tell jokes. The dog who tells the best jokes will get the best score."

A woman said, "How can we tell if one joke is better than the other joke?"

[1]

Rop said, "It's easy to tell which joke is better. If the workers go 'ho, ho' more for one joke, that joke is the better joke."

Then Rop told his joke. This was his joke: "A woman went to see her pal. Her pal was playing checkers with a dog. The woman had never seen a dog that played checkers. So the woman said to her pal, 'That dog is fantastic.'

"Her pal said, 'This dog is not so hot. I beat her 2 of every three games.'"

The workers ho-hoed and ho-hoed.

Rop said, "Let's see you beat that joke, you silly lap dog."

[1]

Rop made Chee so mad that she began to stammer and say odd things.

She said, "I'll lap your slap over never checker playing with a slop rop named yellow teeth."

The workers ho-hoed and ho-hoed. When they stopped going "ho, ho," a woman said to Rop, "We cannot tell if that dog's joke was better than your joke. We think the score is the same."

Rop yelled, "I will get that silly lap dog yet. Let's go into the sleeve-making room for the next meet that we will have."

Chee said, "Fantastic of checkers, with sleeves. OK."

[2]

1

room score coats needle

champ form cutter which

tricking really holler hep

2

A	B
her	herself
him	himself
your	yourself
can	cannot
any	anybody

3

close to shame poke making

4

know another where others

wool ready slapped sleeves

can't else ended from

lap I'll fantastic because

5

Sleeve Slapping

Chee and Rop went into the sleeve-making room of the plant. There Rop said, "I will get the best score for this meet. We will see how fast that lap dog can slap sleeves on coats. The dog that slaps sleeves fastest will get the best score."

Rop handed Chee a needle. Rop said, "Take this needle and get set to go. And don't stab yourself. Ho, ho."

Chee was mad. She held the needle and waited for Rop to say, "Go."

Rop said, "Get set. . . . Go."

Chee went very fast, but she stabbed herself with the needle.

"Ow," she said.

[1]

"Ho, ho," Rop said. "That lap dog just stabbed herself. Ho, ho, ho, hee, hee." As Rop was ho-heeing, he did not see where his needle was going and he stabbed himself. "Ow," he said.

"Ho, hee, hep, hep, hep," Chee said.

Rop yelled, "Stop. This meet is over. I have slapped seven sleeves on coats. So I am the champ, and I get the best score. Let's hear it for me."

"Stop," Chee said. "I have slapped seven sleeves on coats, too. So my score is the same as yours."

Chee was sore where the needle went into her, but she was glad that Rop had stabbed himself, too. Rop said, "Let's go to the room where we form sleeves."

[1]

Chee, Rop, and the others went to the sleeve-forming room. Rop handed Chee shears. Then he handed her a form for making sleeves. He said, "Slap this form on the wool. Then take your shears and cut close to the form. That's how you cut sleeves from wool. Get ready . . . Get set . . . Go."

Chee slapped the form on the wool and began cutting with the shears. She cut very fast. Rop cut fast, too. Rop said, "Don't cut yourself, slow poke."

But Chee did stab herself with the shears. "Ow," she said.

Rop said, "Ho, ho, hee, hep, hep. Ow."

[1]

As Rop ho-hepped, he stabbed himself with the shears.

Then Rop said, "Stop. I made 12 sleeves of wool. I am the fastest sleeve cutter, so I get the best score, and I win."

Chee said, "Hold it. I cut 12 sleeves, too."

The others said that the score was the same for each dog. Rop was getting madder and madder. He said, "This meet has not ended yet."

Rop said, "We will see which of us is the best at tricking the other one. The first dog to get the other dog to say, 'I do,' wins."

Chee said, "This is going to be easy. Ho, ho, hee, hee, hep. You don't know how to make anybody say that."

[2]

Rop got really mad. He said, "Oh, yes I do."

"You said, 'I do,'" Chee said.

One worker said, "Chee wins the meet."

Another worker said, "Chee and Rop are very good. It is a shame that they cannot be pals."

Rop said, "Who said we can't be pals? If we wish to be pals, we will be pals."

"That is the way I see it," Chee said.

From that day on, Chee worked in the sleeve plant. And Chee became pals with Rop.

Rop did not yell at Chee, and Chee did not holler at Rop. They were the best of pals.

[1]

1

dock sold more sailor steel drained
shore beach thin float nail story

2

A	B
your	yourself
seven	seventeen
an	another
some	someone
can	cannot

3

close to lake holes blade
waves while nose side

4

Japan coming turn water
ready ramp slow any
bottom left think from
fog sink swim board
women woman know

5

Sink That Ship

Kit made a boat. She made the boat of tin. The nose of the boat was very thin. Kit said, "I think that this boat is ready for me to take on the lake." So Kit went to the lake with her boat.

Her boat was a lot of fun. It went fast. But when she went to dock it at the boat ramp, she did not slow it down. And the thin nose of the boat cut a <u>hole</u> in the boat ramp.

The man who sold gas at the boat ramp got mad. He said, "That boat cuts like a blade. Do not take the boat on this lake any more. Take it where you will not run into things."

[1]

So Kit did not take her boat to the lake any more. She went to the sea with her boat. She said, "There is a lot of room in the sea. I will not run this boat into any docks."

So Kit went on the sea with her boat. The nose of her boat went into the waves like a blade. Kit's boat went faster and faster. She said, "I am a good sailor."

After a while, she did not see the shore of the sea any more. So Kit went to the left. She said, "I think this is the way back to shore." But now the boat was on its way to Japan.

[1]

A thick fog came in. Kit did not see a thing. She said, "I think I hear waves on the shore."

But Kit did not hear waves on the shore. The waves were coming from the nose of a big ship. That big ship was very near Kit's thin boat. Kit said, "I do hear waves. I must be near a beach."

Just then, a big ship came out of the fog. Kit's thin boat was close to that ship. Kit said, "It is time to turn."

Kit turned the wheel of her boat, but the boat did not turn fast.

[1]

The thin nose of Kit's boat went into the steel side of the big ship. The thin nose cut a hole in the ship.

The women and men on the deck of the ship yelled at Kit, "Stop that, or you will sink this big ship."

Kit said, "I cannot stop. I think my boat likes to cut holes in things."

And Kit's boat cut the biggest hole you have ever seen. The sea began to run into that hole. And the big ship began to sink. The people yelled, "Jump from the side of the ship."

"Swim to my boat," Kit said. And the people did. Seventeen men, 47 women, three dogs, and a pet goat got on Kit's boat.

[1]

An old woman said, "This boat cannot float with all of these people on board."

Just then, the sea began to run over the side of the boat. Kit said, "I can stop this boat from sinking."

She got a hammer and a nail. She held the nail in her left hand and gave it a rap with the hammer. She made a hole in the bottom of the boat. Then she made another hole and another hole.

"What are you doing?" the others asked.

Kit said, "I made holes in the bottom of the boat to drain the water from this boat."

Do you think the water drained from the boat?

You will see in the next story.

[2]

1

goat drain tools shut shore
yum rushed cheered reach

2

A	B
every	everybody
any	anyone
some	somebody
down	downhill

3

holes these likes safe while take

4

head won't melon middle out
bottom water coming bigger
wool filled patted you'll
sniffed chomp sailor's easy
turn steered ordered sleeve

5

The Goat and Kit's Boat

Kit's boat was in the middle of the sea. It had made a hole in a big ship. The big ship went down. Seventeen men, 47 women, three dogs, and a pet goat got in Kit's boat. So Kit made holes in the bottom of the boat to drain the water from the boat.

And the water did begin to drain, but not very fast. Kit said, "These holes are not letting water out faster than the water is coming in the boat. We need a bigger hole in the bottom."

A sailor said, "We left our tools on board the big ship, so we have no way to make bigger holes."

[1]

A man said, "So let's just yell for help. HELP, HELP."

"Shut up," Kit said. "We will get back to shore if we just keep our heads and think of a way to make a big hole that will drain water very fast."

An old woman said, "My pet goat likes to eat tin. Maybe he can eat a hole in the bottom of this tin boat."

"Yes," Kit said. "Let's see what that goat can do." Then she ordered everybody to make room for the goat to eat. "Eat," Kit said.

[1]

And the goat did begin to eat, but it didn't eat the tin boat. It ate a man's wool sleeve. "Stop that," he yelled. "Eat tin, not wool."

Kit said, "Yes, don't let that goat get filled up on wool. It won't have any room for tin."

The old woman who had the pet goat patted the bottom of the tin boat and told the goat, "Yum, yum. Eat this. You'll like it a lot."

The goat sniffed the bottom of the boat and then began to chomp on a sailor's cap. "Take that cap away from the goat," Kit said.

At last, the goat sniffed the bottom of the boat and began to eat the tin.

[2]

The goat made a little hole and kept on eating until that hole was bigger than a melon.

The water rushed out of the boat and everybody cheered. "Let's hear it for the goat," somebody yelled. And everybody cheered again.

Kit said, "There are 65 people in this little boat, and we are safe. But now we must get back to shore."

"That's easy," a sailor said. "Just turn that way and you'll reach shore in a little while."

So Kit steered the boat, and soon it came to the shore. 65 people, three dogs, and one pet goat stepped from the little boat. And everybody was happy.

[2]

1 story painted streak crunch path
smashed bank trench next speed

2

A	B
down	downhill
an	another
some	something
every	everybody

3 nine holes dime waves mile shape

4 front why through tossed asked don't
won't fixing turned leaving from ripping
head closer lower slower know water

5 # Kit's Boat Goes Faster and Faster

This is another story about Kit and her tin boat. Kit had her boat at the dock. She was fixing the hole that the goat made in the boat. She painted her boat green. Then she asked the man who sold gas at the dock, "Where can I get some big rocks?"

The man said, "Why do you need big rocks?"

Kit said, "I will drop them in the front of my boat."

The man asked, "Why will you do that?"

Kit said, "So that my boat will go faster. I don't like boats that go slow."

[1]

The man said, "How will the rocks in the front of your boat make the boat go faster?"

Kit said, "Don't you see? The rocks will make the front of my boat lower than the back of my boat. So my boat will be going downhill. Things go very fast when they go downhill."

The man said, "Ho, ho. Those rocks will just make your boat go slower."

But Kit got rocks and dropped them in the front of her boat. Then she said, "Now it is time to see how fast this boat will run."

[1]

The front of the boat was very low in the water. When Kit let go of the rope, the boat began to go—faster and faster. It went over the waves like a streak. It went faster than the big speed boats. It went faster than any boat on the sea. But it began to turn to the left. It turned more and more. Soon it was going for the dock.

The man on the dock said, "I'm leaving this dock." And he did.

Kit said, "I wish this boat didn't go so fast."

But the boat kept going faster. It came closer and closer to the dock. And then— crunch!—it smashed the dock into little bits.

[1]

Kit said, "This boat does not stop on a dime. In fact, this boat does not stop." The boat kept going. It cut a trench into the side of a hill in back of the dock. It cut a path next to the road. It made a hole in the side of a bank.

At last Kit said, "I think I can make this fast boat stop. I will toss the rocks from the nose of the boat. Then the boat will not be going downhill."

So she began to toss rocks from the boat's nose. She tossed five rocks. Then she tossed another rock, but it was not a rock. It was a bag of gold.

[2]

When the boat went through the bank, nine bags of gold fell in the boat. Kit tossed them from the boat, and the boat stopped. The boat was a mile from the bank.

Then a cop ran up to Kit. She said to Kit, "We have you now, you bank robber."

Kit said, "I did not rob a bank."

The cop said, "Yes, you did. You made this sled for ripping holes in banks."

Kit said, "I am in bad shape, but I think I can fix things."

In the next story, you will see what Kit did.

[1]

1

leave floating sails reached splash shore

2

A	B
up	upside
paint	paintbrush
any	anything
some	somebody

3

why try fly sky

4

shape bribe crime smiled
dive sides bike pike white

5

goodbye light nothing bay yellow
front stepped slid flipped grinned
into fins turned open over
water through hollered herself

Kit Makes Her Boat Lighter

Kit was in bad shape. She said, "I can fix things up."

The cop said, "Do not try to bribe us. This is a crime."

Kit said to her, "I was not trying to bribe you. But you must help me. I need yellow paint."

The cop said, "Why do you need yellow paint?"

Kit said, "Get me the paint and you will see."

So the cop got another cop to run for the paint. The cop stepped in front of Kit and said, "Do not try to leave." When the other cop came back with the can of yellow paint, Kit smiled.

Then she took the lid from the can and began to paint her boat yellow.

[1]

"What are you doing?" the cops asked. "How can it help anything to paint that boat yellow?"

Kit grinned and said, "You will see."

Kit got in the boat, and the boat began to float up into the sky. The cops said, "Do you see what I see? That boat is floating in the sky."

Kit smiled. Then she hollered down to the cops, "Goodbye."

The cops hollered, "Why is that boat floating?"

Kit said, "You see, the boat was green and now it is yellow. Yellow is lighter than green. Now the boat is so light that it floats in the sky."

The boat sailed over a town. Then it turned and sailed over the bay. Then it began to sail over the open sea.

[2]

Kit smiled and said, "Now I will get my can of green paint and make this boat green. Green is not as light as yellow, so this boat will take a dive into the water."

So Kit reached over the side and began to paint. She painted the sides of the boat green, but her paintbrush did not reach the bottom of the boat. So the bottom of the boat was still yellow. That made the bottom lighter than the sides. So the boat turned over.

Kit said, "I think I am going to take a dive into the sea." And she did.

Splash!

[1]

The boat slid into the water upside down. Kit said, "I will flip this boat over and take it back to shore."

She flipped it over. Then she got a grip on the rail. There was a big pike in the bottom of the boat. The pike had yellow paint on its back and on its sides. When the fish flipped its fins, it went into the sky. The fish was very light. The pike floated over the town.

Kit said, "I am going to sell this boat and get a bike. This boat is nothing but a pain."

Then she said to herself, "I can have a lot of fun with a bike. If I get a white bike, it will be very light, so I'll fly over town."

[2]

1

wham   shaft   heap   wait   store
near   boating   stacks   shelf   chin

2

A	B
through	throughout
free	freeway
with	without
every	everything

3

while   home   here   notes   stroked   taken

4

Henry   motor   words   dragged
looked   book   rubbed   fixed
why   cam   because   work   ever
don't   how   glasses   picked   my
nothing   list   front   goodbye
opened   dollars   know   lighter

5

Henry's Hot Rod

Henry had a hot rod. He ran his hot rod very fast down the freeway. But he ran it too fast, and—wham!—there went his cam shaft. Henry said, "Now my hot rod will not go."

A truck came and dragged Henry's rod back to a motor shop. The shop man looked at the motor. Then he rubbed his chin. He said, "I don't think I can get to this job for three weeks. When do you need this heap?"

Henry said, "That hot rod is not a heap. Why can't you get to it now?"

The shop man rubbed his chin. Then he said, "I don't have time."

[1]

The shop man said, "I have three other jobs. When I get them fixed, I can work on your rod."

Henry said, "Where can I take my hot rod to get it fixed now?"

The shop man said, "There is no shop in town that can do the work now. They have lots of jobs."

"Why is that?" Henry asked.

"Because people go too fast when they go down the freeway," the shop man said.

Henry said, "I will not wait. I will fix my motor at home."

"That seems like the best thing to do," the shop man said. "I can't do the job here, so why not do it at home?"

"That is what I will do," Henry said.

[1]

The shop man asked, "Have you ever fixed a motor?"

"No," Henry said. "But that will not stop me. I have looked at my motor, and I don't see why I can't do the job."

The shop man told Henry, "You had better get a book that tells how to fix motors."

"Yes," Henry said.

So the shop man had Henry's hot rod taken to Henry's home. Then Henry went to a book store. When he got there, he asked the woman in the store, "Where are the books on motors?"

[1]

The woman at the book store said, "The books on motors are over there, near the books on boating."

Henry looked at the stacks of books. But Henry did not know how to read. He said to the woman, "I do not have my glasses with me, and I cannot read without them. Can you help me get a book?"

The woman went to the shelf and picked up three books. She handed them to Henry. Then she said, "The green book is not bad. There are things in the red book that are very good. But a lot of people say that the yellow book is the best. It gives lots of notes on how to fix everything in a motor."

[2]

"Where are the notes on the cam shaft?" Henry asked.

The woman said, "There is a list in the front of the book. I'll check it." She did.

She opened the book and handed it to Henry. "Here is everything you need to know," she said.

Henry looked at the words, but he did not know how to read. He stroked his chin and looked at the book. Then he said, "Yes, this book is what I need."

So he gave the woman ten dollars and said, "Thank you." Then he went home with his book.

[1]

LESSON 43

1
bolts   reader   before   steering   clear
which   roar   wish   belts   tore

2

A	B
make	making
dive	diving
trade	trading
smile	smiling
smoke	smoking

3

A	B
him	himself
door	doorway
every	everything

4
Molly   foot   saw   does   whisper   again
motors   why   fixing   press   seals   words
lifted   know   means   tossed   book   some
strip   rested   bottom   steel   through

5

Henry's Sister Helps Him

Henry got a book on fixing motors. Henry went home with the book. He sat in his hot rod and looked at the words in the book, but Henry did not know how to read those words.

Here is what it said in the book: "There are three bolts that hold this end of the cam shaft."

Here is what Henry was reading: "Where are there belts that hold this end for a came shaft."

Henry said, "What does that mean?"

He kept reading. Here is what it said in his book: "When you take the seals from the shaft, you press on them and then lift them from the shaft."

[1]

80 LESSON 43

This is what Henry said when he was reading those words: "Why take and steal I dress and then lifted them of the shaft."

Henry said, "I don't know what this book means." He tossed the book down and said, "I don't need a book to fix this motor. I have seen people work on motors, and I don't think it will be a very big job."

So Henry began to work on his motor. While he was taking some bolts from the motor, a flat strip fell on his foot. "Ow!" he yelled.

[1]

Then he took some other bolts from the motor, and the motor fell on his foot. "Ow," he yelled. He jumped up and down and yelled some more.

His sister, Molly, came through the doorway. "What did you do?" Molly asked. "Why are you yelling?"

"My foot," he yelled. "That motor fell on my foot."

Molly said, "I don't think you know what you are doing. Did you read a book before you began to work on your hot rod?"

"That book does not make sense," Henry said.

Molly got the book and sat next to Henry in his hot rod. She rested the book on the steering wheel. Then she said, "This book seems very clear to me."

[2]

"Will you read it to me?" Henry asked.

"Why not?" Molly said. Then she began to read. "When you work on the cam shaft, take out the 15 bolts from the pan of the motor."

"Where is the pan?" Henry asked.

"I will read and see," his sister said. Molly began to read again. "The pan is on the bottom of the motor. To reach the cam shaft, you must take the pan from the motor."

So Henry took the bolts from the pan. When he had taken the pan from the motor, he saw that there were lots of steel things that made the motor work.

[1]

Henry said to Molly, "Does the book tell which of these things is the cam shaft?"

She said, "I don't know, and I have to go to work. Here is the book. It tells where everything is on the motor. Read the book, and it will tell you what you need to know."

So Molly went to the street and jumped into her hot rod. She grabbed the wheel, and— roar—she tore down the street.

Henry took his book and whispered to himself, "I wish I was a better reader."

[1]

1

dinner   shaft   gear   each
bolted   stick   steel

2

file   these   pile   taken
those   while   broken

3

A	B
time	timing
smoke	smoking
take	taking
ride	riding

4

A	B
in	inside
my	myself
home	homework

5

clothes   done   aside   together   Henry
Molly   trying   motors   tossed   turn
dragging   wham   I've   foot   front   their
fixed   saying   saw   know   slipped
took   does   again   flying   believe   you're

Molly Fixes Her Hot Rod

Henry was trying to fix his motor, but he was not doing very well. He was looking at the words in his book on motors, but Henry did not know what they said. The book said: "To turn a cam shaft, you file each cam."

But this is what Henry said as he was reading: "To turn a cam shaft, you fill each cam."

Henry said, "What does that mean?" He tossed the book aside and said, "That book is not helping me very <u>much</u>. I can do the job myself." So Henry worked and worked.

[1]

After a while, his motor was in little bits. Now he did not have a motor. He had a heap of steel.

"Where is the cam shaft?" he asked as he looked at the big pile of steel.

He picked up a big gear. "Is this a cam shaft?" he asked. He ran his hand over the teeth of the gear. "These things must be the cams," he said.

Henry was looking at the gear when a truck came down the street. The truck was dragging his sister's hot rod.

Molly was mad. She ran over to Henry and said, "Where is that book? My motor broke down and I've got to fix it fast."

[2]

Molly grabbed the book. She ran to her hot rod and began to work.

When it was time for dinner, Molly had fixed her hot rod. She had taken the pan from the motor. She had taken three bent rods from the motor. She had taken those rods to a shop where they were fixed. Then she had slipped them back into the motor and bolted them on the pan.

While she was doing this, Henry was still looking at the gear. He kept saying, "This must be the cam shaft," but he didn't know what to do with it.

[1]

Henry didn't know where the gear came from or how to stick it back into his motor. He didn't even know why the motor needed the gear.

Molly slipped into some clean clothes, ate dinner, and took off in her hot rod. Henry began to bolt his motor back together. When he was done, he said, "There are bits of steel that are left over."

He had a gear, a wheel, three rods, and some little bolts.

"Well," he said, "I think this motor will work well now."

[1]

His hot rod did not run. Bits of steel went flying this way and that way. Smoke came from the motor. Then the motor fell from the hot rod.

Molly had just come home. She said, "I can't believe this mess."

Henry asked, "Will you help me fix my motor?"

"No," she said. "I must do my homework for school. Read your book, and you can fix it."

"But I can't read," Henry said. "You'll have to read to me."

"Not me," she said. Molly went inside. Henry sat looking at his smoking motor. He was very, very sad.

[1]

1

rid   con   paths   trenches   tore   seems

grip   fishing   think   west   tin   aim

2

A	B
him	himself
some	someone
be	become
every	everybody

3

holes   crime   grips   traded   tires   site

pike   fine   these   hike   later

4

ripped   robber   rested   out   began

clock   cash   black   before   happen

ready   done   biggest   together

5

Kit's Trade

Kit said, "I think I will get rid of this boat. It makes ships sink. It has ripped up 2 docks. It has made paths and trenches. It tore holes in the bank, and that is a bad crime."

Kit had a lot to gripe over. So she said, "I will sell the boat." She made a note and stuck it on the side of the tin boat. The note said:

FOR SALE. A TIN BOAT

I WILL TRADE FOR A BIKE.

The con man was in town. He had five tires. Each tire had a hole in it.

[1]

The con man said, "I will sit at this site until I see someone to con." So he sat down on the tires. He was very tired.

While he rested, Kit came up the dock. The con man said to himself, "If I can con this woman, I can get rid of my tires. Then I will get some pike to eat. I like fish."

The con man said, "I have some fine tires if you have something to trade."

Kit said, "I have a boat to trade, but I don't like to trade for tires. I need a bike."

[1]

The con man said, "Trade your boat for these tires. Then you can take these tires and trade them for a bike."

Kit said, "That seems like a good thing to do."

The con man said, "Get a grip on these tires and let's hike down to your boat." So Kit grabbed the tires, and she went with the con man to the boat.

The con man stopped near the boat. He said, "I will not trade five fine tires for this tin heap. I will trade you for three tires."

Kit said, "But this boat is a fine fishing boat. And it will go fast if you drop rocks in the nose."

[1]

Kit told the con man how fast the boat went with the rocks in the nose. She told the con man how the boat went into the bank and came out with nine bags of gold.

The con man began to think this: "I will get the boat, and I will fill the nose with rocks. Then I will become the best bank robber in the West."

But Kit said, "No, I don't think I will trade this boat for the tires. I need a bike."

The con man said, "I will let you have these five fine tires. And I will give you my clock, my cash, and my gold ring."

[2]

So Kit and the con man traded. And later Kit traded the gold ring for a black bike.

The con man got heaps of rocks and dropped them in the nose of the boat. He said, "Now I am ready to become the best bank robber in the West. When the sun comes up in the east, I will aim the boat at the biggest bank in town. Before the day is over, I will have heaps of gold."

When you read the next story, you will see what happens to the con man.

[1]

1

heap   deep   flash   trench
rocket   diver   float   leave

2

space   idea   covered   seal
tug   where   ready   water
began   bits   does   because

3

light   meter   kilometer   taffy
bribe   sink   sea   gripping
faster   fastest   bottom   lifted
waves   spray   flying   zipped
lint   skin   cotton   under

4

The Con Man Gets Cotton Taffy Pike

The con man had traded his clock, his cash, his ring, and five tires with holes in them for Kit's tin boat.

Now the con man was ready to become the best bank robber in the West. He said, "I will pile rocks in the nose of this boat. The more rocks I pile, the faster it will go. So I will make this boat the fastest thing there is."

So the con man slid the boat into deep water near the dock. Then the con man got a big pile of rocks. He dropped ten rocks into the nose of the boat. Then he dropped ten more.

[1]

He said, "Now this boat will go very fast." The nose of the boat was low in the water.

The con man heaped ten more rocks into the nose of the boat. Then he said, "Now this boat will . . . sink." And it did. The nose of the boat went down. And "glub, blub," the boat went to the bottom of the sea.

The con man made a deal with a skin diver. The con man gave the skin diver a coat.

[1]

The skin diver went under the water and lifted the pile of rocks from the boat. Then the boat began to float.

The con man said, "This time I will not heap so many rocks in the nose of this boat." So the con man dropped six rocks into the nose. He hopped into the boat and said, "Now I will fly over the waves."

But the boat did not fly over the waves. It did not go as fast as a sick pike. A seal passed the con man in the water. A tug boat passed him. So did a woman in a row boat.

The con man began to gripe. "Bad, bad," he said. "This boat will not go a kilometer in a year."

[2]

He picked up the paddle and went back to the dock. He heaped ten more rocks in the nose. Then the boat went like a flash. It cut a hole in the water and sent spray flying 200 meters in the air. It went a kilometer in three seconds.

The con man began to smile. "Now I will rip into the biggest bank in town," he said.

The con man turned the boat and went for shore. He was not griping now. He was grinning. And he was gripping the wheel with his hands. He was thinking, "I will slide into that bank and get rich."

[2]

The boat smashed into a dock and tore it to bits. Then it went up the beach. It cut a trench up the hill. It was going as fast as a rocket. The con man said, "I can't tell where the bank is."

Before he had time to think, the boat ripped into the side of a fish-packing plant. The boat made a hole in the other side of the plant. But the con man did not have bags of gold in the boat. He had piles of striped pike. He said, "These fish stink."

[1]

Before he had time to think, the boat ripped into the side of a taffy plant. Now the con man had sticky taffy. And he had a boat filled with taffy pike.

The boat tore a hole into a cotton mill. When it zipped from the mill, the con man had bits of cotton lint on his taffy. He had cotton taffy pike.

The con man said, "I must leave this town and hide from the cops. But I cannot steer this boat. What will I do?"

What do you think he will do?

[1]

1

heaving   wheel   smashed
their   hollered   jail

2

A	B
some	somewhere
any	anything
every	everybody
boat	boatload

3

sticking   must   slid   stared   tossing
taffy   cotton   pants   scare   sticky   factory
striped   press   mill   steering   hide   lint
began   come   space   covered   idea   light

4

A Thing from Space

The con man was zipping here and there in Kit's tin boat. The boat went into a fish-packing plant, into a taffy plant, and into a cotton mill. The con man was a mess. He had a mess of cotton taffy pike in his boat. The steering wheel had taffy on it.

The con man said, "I must go somewhere and hide. I must throw the rocks out of this boat so that it will slow down."

[1]

He began tossing cotton taffy rocks from the nose of the boat. The boat went slower and slower. Then the con man began heaving the pile of pike from the boat. Soon the main street of the town had cotton taffy on it. The boat began to slow down.

The con man said, "Now I will run and hide before the cops come here." But when he went to slip from the boat, he said, "I am sticking to the seat. This taffy will not let go of me."

[1]

The cops and their nine dogs ran up to the con man. The man from the dock ran up to him. The man hollered, "That is the man who smashed my dock into bits."

The woman from the fish-packing plant ran up to the con man. The fish packer said, "That is the man who made a hole in my plant. He zipped away with a boatload of striped pike."

The man from the taffy factory came running up the street. He yelled, "Stop that man. He tore a hole in my plant and stole a boatload of taffy."

[2]

The woman who ran the cotton mill was next. She was really mad. She said, "This is the man who broke my cotton-making press."

The cops yelled, "We have you now. We will send you to jail for the rest of your life."

The dogs said, "Ooowww, ooowww."

The con man said, "Bad, bad. I don't like jails. I must get out of here fast."

Then the con man got an idea. He said to himself, "I must look funny. I am covered with cotton lint."

Slowly the con man began to stand up. The taffy was sticking to his pants, and he had torn a big hole in his pants. The con man said, "Do not bother me. This is a space ship. And I come from space."

[2]

The dogs stopped going, "Ooowww." The cops stopped running. The other people stopped hollering. They stared at the con man. Then the woman from the cotton mill said, "It must be from space. I have never seen anything like it before."

The man from the dock said, "It is more like a bag of cotton than anything I have seen."

The man from the taffy plant said, "I am leaving. I don't think I like things from space."

The con man said to himself, "Ho, ho. They think that I am from space. I think I will scare them. Ho, ho."

What do you think the con man will do next?

[2]

1 near   rain   what   gold

leave   splash   drain   before

2

A	B
every	everybody
an	another
every	everything
him	himself

3 sticking   melt   fate   teller   ray

scare   smashed   striped   lint   cotton

middle   didn't   plop   before   hospital

skin   robbery   spot   pick   space

light   nose   idea   covered

4 # The Bank Robbery Fails

The con man made everybody think that he was from space. He was a big mass of cotton lint. The cotton lint was sticking to taffy. And the taffy was sticking to the con man's skin. It was sticking to everything. The con man said to himself, "I will give these people the scare of their lives."

He held up his hands and said a deep "Rrrrrr."

Three dogs went, "Ooooww," and ran down the street.

Then the con man said, "I am from space, and I will get you."

The dock man said, "I'm going to run to the sea and dive in." That is what he did. So did the people from the plants.

[2]

The cops said, "Let's not make this space thing mad." They smiled at him.

The con man said, "Rrrrrr. I will get you." He began to go for the cops.

The cops said, "We had better leave this spot." And they did. They ran down the street and—splash!—they dived into the sea.

The con man was standing in the middle of the street. Nobody was near him. He said,

"Wow! This is fun. I think I'll go into the bank and see if I can pick up some bags of gold."

[1]

So the con man went into the bank. The con man didn't see well. His nose was a mass of cotton lint. So the con man didn't see a striped pike in front of the bank.

Slip! There went the con man when he stepped on the pike. Plop! That was the con man hitting the street with his seat.

"Bad, bad," the con man griped. He picked up the striped pike and flipped it into the street. Then he went into the bank.

He went up to the teller in the bank. The con man said to her, "Rrrrr. Give me gold, or I will zap you with my ray gun."

[2]

The teller said, "Yes, yes. Take the gold, but do not zap me with your ray gun."

So the con man got gold. He said, "I have more gold than I can hold."

He lifted three big bags of gold and left the bank. He went into the street. He did not see the striped pike in the middle of the street.

Slip! That was the con man. Plop! That was the con man's seat hitting the street. Plop, plop, plop! Those were the bags of gold landing on the con man.

[1]

"Bad, bad," the con man griped. He grabbed the bags and began to stand up. But just then a drop of rain hit the con man on the hand. Then another drop landed on his coat. Then five more hit him. The con man said, "I must hide before the rain makes me wet. If I get wet, the taffy will melt. Then the lint will not stick. And then everybody will see that I am not from space. They will see that I am the con man."

The con man began to run with the bags of gold. But the bags were not light, and the con man did not run very fast. He said, "Bad, bad. This rain is making my plan go down the drain."

[2]

1   sore   moaned   what

     raining   sneak   licked   jailer

2   laugh   walk   hair   plop   landed

     idea   space   bank   pale   coming

3   busted   liked   taffy   trick   slide

     three   slippery   trying   dying   tired

4

The Con Man Gets Busted

It was raining and the con man was griping about the rain. He said, "My plan is going down the drain."

He was trying to run with the three bags of gold, but they were not light and he did not run fast. The cotton in his hair was running down his nose. He did not see where he was going. He slipped on a pile of slippery pike and—plop, plop, plop!—the con man hit the street, and the three bags of gold landed on the con man.

[1]

A little boy was standing near the con man. The boy said, "You are not from space. I can see that you are just a wet man."

The lint was sliding from the con man's hair, from his hands, from his nose, and from his coat. The rain was coming down very fast, and the con man was very, very wet.

A dog ran up to the con man and began to lick the taffy from his hand. "Don't bite me," the con man said. And the dog did not bite. It licked and licked. It liked the taffy. Then three cats came up to the con man. They began to lick the taffy.

[2]

Then five dogs and nine goats came over and began licking taffy.

"I don't like this," the con man said. He was trying to get up. He said, "I must get to the other side of the street." But he slipped on a striped pike and—plop!—he was back on his seat in the street.

The cops ran up to the con man. "Don't try to leave," they said. "We've got you now, you slippery sneak."

"Oooooooww," the con man moaned. "Now I will have to go to jail."

[1]

And that is just what happened. The cops and nine dogs led the con man to the jail. They locked the con man up. Then they sent the gold back to the bank.

The con man said, "I hate jails. I must get out of here." He began to think of ways to trick the cops into letting him go.

Then he got an idea. He began moaning, "Oh, oh. I am sick. I am pale. I am not well."

The jailer came to the other side of the door. She said, "If you are sick, we will have to send you to the hospital."

"Yes, yes," the con man said. "I think I am dying. That's how sick I am."

[2]

The jailer yelled for a cop. "Get this man to the hospital," she said.

The cop said, "Do you think this man is faking?"

"No," the jailer said. "This man is very cold. And he seems to be very pale. I don't think he's faking. I think he's sick."

The con man was smiling to himself. He was thinking, "I may seem sick, but I am still in fine shape for conning jailers."

So the jailer opened the door, and the cop said, "Well, if he's not acting, we had better take him to the hospital."

You will see what happened when you read the next con man story.

[2]

1 leaves shade holes sneak
wish waited creep lower

2 buy hear bend luck drum
here happy mother brothers come

3 anything sisters digging mine
joke came laugh hotter dusty
runner silver stayed walked

The Bug That Dug

There was a bug. That bug liked to dig. He dug and dug. His mother said, "Why do you keep digging? The rest of us bugs eat leaves and sit in the shade. But you dig and dig."

"When I dig, I feel happy," the digging bug said. "I like to make holes."

So he made holes. When he stopped digging, he was dusty. His brothers and sisters said, "You are a mess. You have dust on your back. What are you doing?"

The bug said, "When I dig, I feel happy." And so that bug dug and dug.

[1]

Then something happened. The days began to get hotter and hotter. The sun was so hot that the other bugs said, "We cannot stay here. It is too hot. We must go to a spot that is not so hot."

They walked here and there, but they did not find a spot that felt cool. Then they came to a big hole in the side of a hill. They said, "Let's go down this hole. It looks cool inside."

The bugs went inside the hole. Then the mother bug stopped. She said, "Did you hear that? I hear something in this hole."

The other bugs stopped. Then one of them said, "Yes, I hear something. I think I hear digging."

[2]

So the bugs began to sneak down the hole. Soon they came to a bend in the hole. The mother bug said, "Stay here and I will check out the digging." The other bugs waited, and the mother bug began to creep to the bend. Then she stopped.

What do you think she saw? She saw a dusty bug digging and digging. She said, "So this is where you go when you dig."

The dusty bug stopped digging. He said, "Yes, this is my mine. I come here to dig every day."

[1]

"What are you digging for?" the mother bug asked.

"I mine gold," the bug said.

The mother bug began to laugh. She laughed and laughed. She said, "That is a joke. A bug digging for gold. Did you ever hear anything so funny?"

The dusty bug said, "Don't make fun of my gold mine. If I don't find gold in this hole, I will get some silver."

"Silver," the mother bug said and began to laugh again. When she stopped laughing, she said, "There is no silver in these hills."

[1]

The bug said, "I'll bet you that I will have some silver before the sun sets."

"That is a bet," his mother said. "This mine is a dud. I'll bet you a dollar that you won't have silver before the sun sets."

Then the dusty bug began to scream, "Leave this mine. I did not ask you to come here. So get out."

He ran to the other bugs. "Go home," he said. "Leave this mine."

But the other bugs said, "No. It is too hot in the sun. We like it here where it is cool."

[1]

The dusty bug said, "Pay me a dime, or leave my mine."

So each of the bugs gave the dusty bug a dime. Then the dusty bug went to the mother bug. He said, "When we bet, you said that I will not have silver when the sun sets, but I have lots of silver in my hand."

The mother bug was mad, but she said, "You win." She gave him a dollar.

But then the dusty bug said, "Now you must pay a dime if you wish to stay in my mine." So the mother bug gave the dusty bug a dime.

The bugs stayed in that mine until the sun was lower and the air was not so hot.

[2]

1

ou

A	B
out	sound
our	mouth
loud	outside

2

gone clerk burp cash one buy
smell walk such tired door
another laugh handed rotten
side joking rusty eating
grinned chomp three smiled

3

The Bug and the Pickle Tub

The dusty bug was resting in his mine. It was hot outside. He had a rusty shovel. He had been digging with the shovel, but now he was tired. He said, "I need to eat. I like dill pickles, but I don't have any dills."

He tossed the shovel to one side. Then he came out of his mine. The sun was very hot. The bug went to a store. Then he picked up a tub of pickles. He said to the clerk, "Will you bill me for these dill pickles?"

The clerk said, "No, we do not bill for pickles. You must pay cash in this store."

[1]

The bug said, "I don't have cash with me. But if you send me a bill, I will pay for it."

The clerk said, "You did not hear me. I said that we do not bill for dill pickles."

The bug said, "That's fine with me. Now that I smell these pickles, I can tell that they are rotten."

"They are not rotten," the clerk said. "They are the best pickles in town."

The bug began to laugh. Then he said, "These pickles are so bad that they will make you sick if you eat them."

[1]

The clerk ran over to the bug. The clerk said, "Give me one of those pickles. I'll show you that they are good."

The bug handed the pickle to the clerk. The clerk chomped on the pickle. Then the clerk smiled. "That dill is fine," she said.

The bug said, "You must have picked a good dill, but some of these dills are bad." The bug picked up a big dill and began to chomp on it. He puckered his mouth. Then he said, "That dill is bad."

[1]

The clerk reached into the pickle tub and got a big pickle. She ate it in three chomps. Then she grinned. "My, my," she said. "That was a good pickle. In fact, that was the best dill I have had in some time."

The bug dug into the tub and got a big dill. He chomped it down. Then he said, "That dill was a dud. It was so bad that I feel sick."

The clerk said, "You don't know a good dill when you eat one." So the clerk dug a big dill from the tub. She smelled it. "Good, good," she said. Then she ate it.

[1]

When the clerk was done eating, she said, "My, my, did you ever see such a good dill?"

The dusty bug said, "I think you are joking. You say that the dills are good, but the dills that I eat are bad."

The clerk dug another dill from the tub. She handed it to the bug and said, "Try this dill. It is not a dud. I'll tell you that."

So the bug ate the dill. Then he smiled. He said, "You are right. That dill is just fine. See if you can give me another one that is good."

"That's easy," the clerk said. She got another dill and handed it to the bug. The bug chomped it down.

[2]

Then the bug said, "You're good at digging out the best dills. That dill was the best yet. See if you dig out another good one."

Soon the bug had eaten every pickle in the tub. Then he said, "Well, I think I'll go back to my mine. I don't think I'll buy any pickles today. So you don't have to send me a bill."

The clerk looked at the bug. Then she looked at the tub. She said, "What is this? The dills are gone."

The dusty bug smiled from the door of the store. Then he said, "Burp." And he went back to his mine.

[2]

1 ou

A	B
sound	mouth
hour	house
found	outside
cloud	loudly

2

orange floor home hear rip

tug bing dinging bop bus

dropped wife liked woman before

clock deer cheer drink tape

saying maker didn't fixing bay

bees holding speak really gone

3 # The Old Clock Maker

The old clock maker liked to work with plants when he wasn't working with clocks. He had lots of plants in back of his home. Every day after work, he dressed in a bib and went to dabble with his plants. While he dabbled, he talked. He didn't hear himself, so he didn't know that he was saying things very loudly. When he came to a plant that did not have buds, he said, "This plant is a dud, because it doesn't have one bud."

[1]

One day, he was dabbling and talking when his wife came out. She said, "A woman is here. Can you make a bid on fixing a clock?"

The old clock maker did not hear her. The clock maker said, "I do not have a rip in my bib."

His wife said, "I did not say 'bib,' I said 'bid.' A woman needs a bid. Can you tell her how much she will have to pay?"

"I'm not going to the bay," the clock maker said. "I'm going to stay here with the bees and my plants."

"Come with me," his wife said. "I will let you speak to the woman." So she led the old clock maker inside.

[2]

A woman was standing near the door. She was holding a big clock. The woman said, "When this clock works, a deer runs out every hour, and the clock goes, 'ding, ding.' But the clock does not work. The deer does not come out, and the clock goes, 'bing, bing.'"

The clock maker said, "I'm glad to meet you, Mrs. Bing Bing. What can I do for you?"

The clock maker's wife said to the woman, "You will have to yell if you want him to hear what you say."

So the woman yelled. She told the clock maker about the deer, and about the dinging and binging.

[1]

The clock maker said, "I've never seen a clock that cheered every hour. I've seen clocks with a deer that comes out every hour, but never a clock that cheers."

"No, no," the woman yelled. "This clock has a deer."

The clock maker said, "How does that work? Does the deer make the cheer?"

The woman yelled, "There is no cheer, just a deer."

"Oh," the clock maker said.

[1]

The clock maker took off his big bib. Then he said, "When did the clock stop working?"

The woman yelled, "When I dropped it."

The clock maker said, "You must not bop clocks. The clock is a dud now."

"I didn't bop it," the woman yelled. "I dropped it. Drop, drop, drop."

The clock maker said, "So your clock has a leak and it goes, 'drop, drop, drop.' Take a bit of tape and dab it on the hole. That will stop the leak."

"No," the woman yelled. "My clock does not leak. It is a bad clock. It doesn't work."

"Let me see that clock," the clock maker said.

[2]

He grabbed the clock and dropped it. The clock made a loud sound when it hit the floor. The deer fell out. A spring went, "bop." The clock went, "bing, bing, ding."

The clock maker said, "That clock is broken. Let me make a bid on fixing it for you."

The woman was really mad. She said, "You dropped that clock. It was not in such bad shape before you did that."

The clock maker said, "I will fix the clock for eleven dollars."

The woman said, "Good."

[1]

1

house   brush   room   deer
sound   dear   loudly   paint   dingers

2

parts   girl   held   dong   ding
fine   well   orange   floor

3

working   can't   gone   again
bobbed   dabbed   slapped   frog
hands   din   miles   room
fellow   yellow   looked   himself
wiped   why   dear   stand

4

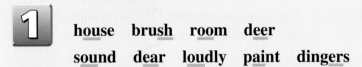

The Deer That Bobbed Like a Frog

The clock maker gave a bid on the clock that he had dropped. He made a bid of eleven dollars. Then he took the clock to his work room. In that room he had lots of clocks. Every hour, the clocks went, "dong, dong" and "ding, ding." But the clock maker did not hear them.

In the work room, the clock maker had a bin of parts from other clocks. He also had a lot of tools for fixing clocks.

The clock maker held the clock with the deer. He said, "I will have to paint this clock." So he got a brush and dabbed paint on the clock.

[1]

He made the clock orange. Then he dabbed paint on the deer. He made the deer yellow.

Then he went to his bin of old clocks to look for one that had a good deer. He looked and looked. Then he began to talk to himself. He said, "This is bad. I made a bid on fixing this clock, but I cannot see another clock with a working deer. The best I can see is a clock with a working frog. That frog comes out every hour and bobs up and down."

The clock maker took the parts from the clock with the frog and slapped them into the clock with the deer.

[2]

At the end of an hour, the deer came out and bobbed up and down like a frog. The clock maker was happy.

Next the clock maker said, "Now I will fix the clock so that it goes, 'ding, ding.' "

Five clocks in his bin had good dingers, but the clock maker did not hear the sounds they made. He picked a clock that did not go, "ding." That clock went "dong, dong."

[1]

He took the bell from the clock that went "dong." He said, "This part will work fine in the clock with a deer." So he slapped the bell into the deer clock. Then he said, "Now the woman will have a clock that works well."

The clock maker wiped his hands on his bib. Then he took the clock to the woman. He said, "Here it is."

The woman looked at the clock. Just then, the bell went, "dong, dong." The woman said, "What a sound! You can hear this clock for miles."

Then the deer came out of the clock.

[2]

The woman said, "What is that deer doing? It is bobbing up and down like a frog. Why is this clock orange? And why is the deer yellow?"

"Yes," the clock maker said, "He is a dear fellow."

"Not fellow," the woman said. "Yellow. Yellow. Why is it yellow?"

"You don't have to yell," the clock maker said. "I can hear you. I like it yellow, too."

The woman got so mad that she began to yell. "This clock looks bad. When you gave a bid, you said, 'I will fix the clock.' But now this clock is a dud."

The clock maker said, "Yes, that clock is good."

The woman said, "Here. You may keep this clock. I can't stand it." She tossed the clock down, and it broke into parts.

So the clock maker left with the parts of the clock. He said, "That woman keeps dropping the clock. But I'll fix it for her again."

[2]

1

reached   ouch   painted   toad

outside   shook   beads   found

2

already   garden   parts   collar

bopped   dent   bent   shake

3

gone   doesn't   opened   orange   haven't

girl   weeds   know   suddenly   antlers   blip

yellow   bleep   busted   finger   broken

across   took   one   alligator

An Alligator Clock

The clock maker had painted a clock orange. He had made the deer yellow. He had fixed the deer so that it bobbed up and down like a frog. When the clock maker took the clock to the woman, the woman got very mad. She tossed the clock down. The clock maker took the broken clock back to his shop. He was going to fix it again.

He had just put his work bib on when his wife came in. She said, "Did you just come in?"

"Yes," the clock maker said, "I can grin." And he did.

His wife shook her head. Then she said, "A little girl is outside. She wants to know if she can pick weeds in your garden."

[2]

The clock maker said, "There are no seeds in my garden. The plants are just getting buds. They won't have seeds before the end of summer."

"Not seeds," his wife said. "Weeds. The girl wants to pick weeds."

"Why does she want to plant weeds?" the clock maker asked.

His wife was getting mad. She said, "I will tell her that she can pick weeds. If she does a good job, I will pay her one dollar."

"That's fine," the clock maker said. "But you don't have to holler."

[1]

His wife walked from the room. Then the old clock maker wiped his hands on his bib. "Time to go to work," he said.

He grabbed the broken deer clock and began to set it on his work table when, suddenly, "bam." He dropped the clock. That bent the yellow deer and made a dent in the side of the clock. And the bell did not work. It went "blip, bleep."

"Oh, my," the old man said. "Now I have a big job." He went to the bin. He picked up a string of beads. "Good," he said. "I can string these beads over the side of the clock. The beads will hide the dent in the side."

[1]

Then the clock maker looked for a good deer in his bin. But every deer was broken or bent. "Well, well," he said. The clock maker rubbed his big bib. Then he said, "I may have a good clock under the bin."

So the old clock maker looked under the bin. He came up with a dusty old clock. He said, "This clock is busted, but I think it is the clock I need."

The clock maker began to shake the dust from the clock when the clock door opened and out came an alligator. It ran across the front of the clock and bit the clock maker's finger.

[1]

The clock maker said, "Ouch! This clock doesn't have a deer in it. It has an alligator."

The old man sat down and began to think. "How will I fix that deer clock?" he said to himself. Then he jumped up and said, "I've got it. I will fix the alligator so that it looks like a deer. I will put antlers on it."

The clock maker reached inside the clock and grabbed the alligator. He got some yellow paint and dabbed paint on the alligator. "Not bad," said the old clock maker. "That alligator looks more like a deer already."

[1]

Then the clock maker took the antlers from the broken deer and stuck them on the alligator. "Good," the clock maker said. Then he slapped the alligator into the deer clock. He set the hands of the clock at three o'clock.

Suddenly the bell went, "Blub, blub." At the same time, the alligator came out. It bobbed up and down like a frog. It bit the old clock maker's finger. Then it ducked inside the clock.

The old man said, "That clock looks just fine now. The woman will never know that I made another deer from this clock. She will be glad to pay eleven dollars to get this fine clock back."

So the old clock maker took the clock to the woman.

[2]

1 ar

A	B
arm	are
part	yard
hard	garden
farm	barking

2 branch around jailer while
sounded toad cleaned sailing
scream shout horned beads told

3 birds want girl third roof stayed
bobbed blow wanted door buy
shape I've they've busted frog
dusty took antlers rapped
eleven garden already

4 # The Clock in the Tree

The clock maker had taken an alligator from a dusty old clock and had slapped it into the deer clock. The alligator was yellow, and it had antlers. The old man said, "This clock looks just like it did before."

So the clock maker took the clock to the woman. The clock maker rapped on her door. The woman came to the door. "What do you want?" she said.

"Here it is," the clock maker said. He held up the alligator clock. "This clock is fixed up as good as ever."

The woman looked at the clock and said, "Oh, no. I don't want to buy dusty clocks with beads on them. I had a good clock, and you busted that clock. Now you are selling old junk clocks."

"Yes," the old clock maker said. "It looks just as good as ever. Here, hold it while I set the hands."

Before the woman was able to back away, the clock maker handed her the clock and began to set the hands. As soon as the hands

[1]

were set for five o'clock, the clock made a loud sound. "Blip, blop," sounded the bell.

[1]

And here came the alligator. It bobbed up and down. It bobbed this way and that way. It ran around the front of the clock. Then it bit the woman's finger.

"Ouch!" yelled the woman. She dropped the clock. The alligator grabbed her foot. The paint on the alligator was wet, and now the woman had a big yellow spot on her foot.

Now the alligator began to bite the woman's leg. "Ouch, ouch," the woman yelled. "What is that thing? It looks like a horned toad."

"Stop dropping that clock," the old man said. "You will make more dents in it."

[2]

The woman yelled, "Make that horned toad stop biting me, or I will bust that clock."

"Yes," the clock maker said, "there was some dust on the clock, but I cleaned it up."

The alligator kept biting the woman's leg, so the woman stepped on the clock. "Bing, bong, dong," went the bell. Beads went sailing this way and that. Then the alligator was still. The woman said, "Get that clock out of here."

"Yes, it's a fine deer," the clock maker said. "But I think you bent the clock out of shape when you stepped on it."

[1]

The woman yelled, "I don't want that clock. Take it and get out of here."

The clock maker said, "Yes, I like that deer, too. But you don't have to shout. Pay me the eleven dollars, and I'll be on my way this day."

"I'll pay you this," the woman said. She picked up the clock and tossed it into a tree. It stuck on a branch. A little yellow bird came and sat on the alligator's antlers. Another bird came and sat on the hour hand.

"Look at that," the woman said. "Those birds like that clock. They think it is a bird's nest."

The clock maker said, "Yes, it is the best. I just hope those birds can tell time."

[2]

The woman said, "For some time, I've wanted to get those birds into my tree, but this is the first time they've come to the tree. Thank you. How can I pay you for that?"

"Hand me eleven dollars, and I'll be on my way this day," the clock maker said. So the woman gave the clock maker eleven dollars, and the clock maker went home.

The woman stayed in her yard and looked at the birds. The birds sat on the alligator. And when the wind began to blow, the alligator bobbed up and down like a frog.

[1]

1

ar

A	B
start	sharp
smart	barking
farmer	hard

2

jailer scream outside chest years
pounded goat brains
shouted helper stuck

3

two nurse around anything leave
room hospital want girl taking
what's doctor ready pretty because
fakes suddenly smiled trick
else floor snapping growled foxy

4

The Con Man Acts Like a Dog

When we left the con man, he was in the hospital. He had told the cops and the jailer that he was sick. He really wasn't sick. He was just playing sick. But the cop took him to the hospital. The cop went up to a nurse and said, "Nurse, I have a sick man. He needs help."

The nurse said, "We will fix him up fast." She had the con man sit on a cart. Then she took the con man to a room.

As soon as she left the room, the con man darted for the door. He peeked outside. But the cop was standing near the door. "Nuts," the con man said. "I will try the window."

[1]

He darted to the window. He grabbed the handles and opened it wide. Then he looked out. There were bars on the window. "Nuts," the con man said.

He sat on the bed and said to himself, "I must think of a trick that will get me out of here." Suddenly he jumped up. "I've got it," he yelled. Then he began to bark like a dog. He had a plan.

The nurse came running in. "What's that barking?" she asked.

The con man got down on the floor and growled at her. "Rrrrr." Then he began snapping his teeth.

"Oh!" she screamed. "This man has gone mad."

[1]

The cop ran in. The con man barked at him. The cop said, "I think this man is ready for the rest home. He is not well."

Three people came in and grabbed the con man. They took him to a bus. The bus took him to the rest home. The con man smiled to himself on the way to the rest home. He said to himself, "My plan is working. They will take me to the rest home. When I get there, I will tell the doctors that I feel better. They will let me leave the home. I am very, very smart."

When the bus got to the rest home, the people led the con man into a big room. Then a doctor came in.

[2]

A woman said, "Here he is, Doc. He thinks he's a dog."

The doctor said, "Thank you. We will give him the best of help."

The three people left, and as soon as they did, the con man said, "Doctor, I feel better now. I don't think I'm a dog any more. Why don't you let me go home?"

The doctor said, "So you don't feel like a dog. What do you feel like?"

The con man said, "I feel like a con man."

So the doctor said, "You think you're a con man, do you?" She began taking notes on her pad.

"Yes," the con man said. "I think I'm a con man because I am a con man."

[2]

"I see," the doctor said, and she took more notes. "When did you start feeling like a con man?"

The con man was starting to get mad. "I've felt like a con man for years and years."

The doctor said, "Did you feel like a con man before you felt like a dog?"

"Yes, I am a con man," the con man said.

The doctor said, "Have you ever felt like anything else—a goat, or a farmer?"

"Look," the con man said, "I never think I'm anything but a con man. I out fox people. That's what I do."

"You feel pretty foxy, do you?" the doctor asked.

"Yes," the con man said. He stuck out his chest. "I am the king fox."

The doctor called for two helpers. She said, "Lock this man up. He thinks he's a fox now."

[2]

1 pounded   march   brains   heave   charge
found   garden   easy   around   whatever

2 sir   private   squad   charge   President
foxy   muttered   okay   Washington

3 escaped   smiled   maybe   wait
window   along   helpers   mean
our   outside   ground   hadn't
people   walked   talk   guy
two   nurse   want   came   odd

4
The Con Man Meets the President

The con man had told the doctor that he was very foxy. The doctor had two helpers lock up the con man. The doctor said, "That man thinks he's a fox now."

So the helpers took the con man to a little room at the far end of the yard. They said, "You will like this room. You will have a good time."

The con man said, "I am too smart for you. I will get out of this room before the sun sets."

But the sun set, and the con man hadn't found a way to get out of the room. He pounded on the floor. He tried to get out the window. But the window had bars on it. And the bars did not bend.

[2]

At last, the con man sat down on the bed. He said, "I will have to think with my brains. There must be some way to get out of here."

Somebody said, "It is easy to get out of here."

The con man looked around the room, but he did not see anybody. The con man said, "Maybe I am out of it. I am hearing people talk."

Just then the con man saw a foot under the bed. The con man grabbed the foot and gave it a heave. Out came a man. He was smiling. He said, "Hello. My name is President Washington. I am the father of our country."

[1]

The con man said, "You seem really odd. I do not want to share this room with you."

The man stood up. He said, "If you keep talking like that, you will end up in front of a firing squad."

"Stop it," the con man said. "You are not President Washington, and there are no firing squads around here."

The man said, "If you are going to be mean, I won't tell you how to get out of this room." The man walked to the far side of the room.

[1]

The con man said, "Okay, I won't make fun of you if you tell me how to leave this room."

The man walked back and stared at the con man. Then he said, "The best way to leave this room is to open the door and walk out. Ho, ho."

The con man said, "That's not very funny, president."

The man said, "But wait. I was just kidding you. There is a way to leave this room. Here's how it works: You hide under the bed with me. When the helpers come into the room, they look around and they don't see anybody. They say, 'We had better go for help.' They leave the door open, and they run from the room. Then we get out from under the bed, and we run outside."

[2]

The con man smiled. He said, "That is a fine plan."

The man said, "But remember, the plan is mine. Mine. And I am the president. So I will be in charge when we escape from this room."

The con man was getting mad, but he said to himself, "I must play along with this guy."

So the con man said, "Okay, you are in charge. I will do whatever you say."

"Good," the man said. "You may be a private in my army."

"No," the con man said. "I don't want to be a private."

[1]

The president jumped up and down on the bed. Then he started to scream. He yelled, "I won't let you leave this room if you won't be a private in my army."

"Okay, okay," the con man said. "I'll be a private."

The man said, "That's better. Now start to march, private."

The con man muttered to himself, but he began to march.

He marched and marched and marched. Then the president said, "Now remember, private, when we make our escape, I am in charge. You must do everything I say."

"Yes, sir," the con man said.

[1]

1

wheat   shouted   alarm   whispered

yard   without   nearby   eaten

darted   wait   sneeze   orders   loose

2

love   quick   right   who   check

peeked   cakes   pressed   while   button

3

don't   wants   foot   because

talking   take   tried   tired

front   escaped   show   rest

private   across   sir   grove

hiding   yum   remember   fool

4

A Foxy Escape, Part 1

The con man was in a room with a man who said that he was President Washington. President Washington said that he was in charge of their escape. The con man was just a private in his army.

The next day, the president said, "Soon they will come around to feed us. When we hear them at the door, we will zip under the bed. And we will wait without making a sound. Remember to do everything I say, because I don't want anything to mar my plans."

"Yes, sir," the con man said. He was very tired. He had marched and marched. He had taken lots of orders from the president.

[1]

Just then, there was a sound outside the door. "Quick," the president said. "Dart under the bed. And don't let your feet show."

The con man darted under the bed. The president darted under the bed. Then the president whispered, "There is dust under this bed, and dust makes me sneeze."

The con man whispered, "Don't sneeze."

"Shut up, private," whispered the president.

The door opened. The con man peeked out and saw two legs walking across the room. Then he saw two more. "Where are they?" a man asked.

"Hee, hee," the president whispered. "I can fool them every time."

[1]

A woman said, "We had better sound the alarm. It looks as if they escaped."

The first man said, "But how did they get loose? There is no way out of this room."

"I don't know," the woman said. "But they are not here. I'll sound the alarm. You check around the yard. Maybe they are hiding nearby."

The con man saw the legs leave the room. "Hee, hee," the president said. He slipped out from under the bed. So did the con man.

Then the president ran to the table. The helpers had left food on the table. The president said, "Oh, boy! Wheat cakes. I just love wheat cakes. Yum, yum."

[1]

"Come on," the con man said. "We don't have time to eat now. We must escape."

"Private," the president said, "sit down and eat your wheat cakes. And if you don't do it right now, I won't let you have any butter for your wheat cakes."

The con man said, "But, president, sir, the helpers will be back soon. We must leave."

"No, private," said the president. "They won't be back for a while. And you will see them coming, because you will be standing near the door as you eat your wheat cakes. And you will be keeping a sharp look out."

"Yes, sir," the con man said. He took his plate of wheat cakes and stood near the door.

[2]

The con man had just begun to eat when the president said, "Now we must go."

The con man said, "But I just started to eat."

"You are a very slow eater, private," the president said. "I have just eaten three plates of wheat cakes."

So the con man dropped his plate. Then he began to run with the president. They ran across the yard. They ran to the front gate. The gate was locked.

"Hide in that grove of trees," the president said. So the con man ducked into the grove of trees.

[1]

The president said, "Now I will go out and get the man to open the gate for us."

"That man won't open the gate. He won't let us just walk out of here."

"Private, shut up."

The president walked from the grove. He walked up to the gate. He stuck his foot in the gate. Then he began to scream, "Oh, my foot. It is stuck in the gate. Open the gate quickly."

The man who ran the gate pressed the button and the gate opened. Then the president began to yell. "Is there anybody around here who can help me get my foot loose? Is there anybody hiding in a grove of trees?"

The con man said, "That's me. He wants me to come out and help him."

"I'll be right there," the con man shouted.

[2]

1 oul could would should
couldn't wouldn't

2 nearest started loudly white shouted
steered please tooted main shack

3 full first bridal jogged green some
can't right they'll idea waved
spray hotel stared yokels jacket
company follow skipped two
steered grove love quick

A Foxy Excape, Part 2

The con man ran from the grove of trees. He jogged up to the president. The president smiled and said, "You see, private, the gate is open. And we are free. Let's run down that road before these yokels come after us."

So the con man and the president ran down the road. The people from the rest home ran up to the gate. They said to the gate man. "Did you open the gate and let those men escape?"

"Yes, I did," the gate man said. "But the first man had his foot stuck in the gate. He was in pain."

"You yokel," the people said. Six people began to run after the con man and the president.

[1]

"I'm getting tired," the con man said. "Let's stop and rest."

"Shut up, private," the president said. "You'll never become a major thinking the way you do."

"I don't want to become a major," the con man said. "I just want to get out of here."

"Then do what I say," the president shouted. "We're going back to the rest home. Follow me."

"What?" the con man asked. "We can't go back. They'll get us."

"No, no," the president said. "They don't think that we will go back. That is the last spot they will look. Just do as I say, private."

[1]

So the president and the con man began to sneak back to the gate. The gate was open, and the gate man was looking the other way. So the con man and the president skipped by him. They went to a shack near the grove of trees.

In the shack were white jackets. The president handed a jacket to the con man. He said, "Private, slip into this jacket. Then they will think that you work here."

When the con man and the president were dressed in white jackets, they left the shack. The president led the way to the main office. He walked up to the woman and said, "We have a lead on those two men who escaped. We need a car to get them. They are at a farm not far down the lane."

[2]

The woman said, "Take the green car in front of the office."

So the con man and the president got in the green car. The president said, "You must drive. I am the president, and presidents don't drive cars. They have privates who drive for them."

"Yes, sir," the con man said. He started the car and went down the lane to the gate. The gate man waved at them and opened the gate. The car went down the road. It went past the people who were looking for the con man and the president. The con man tooted the horn. The people waved at the car.

[1]

The con man steered the car to the nearest town. Then the president said, "Stop in front of the best hotel in this town. I am tired of driving. I must rest."

"But—" the con man started to say.

"Shut up, private."

"Yes, sir."

So the con man stopped the car in front of the best hotel. The president smiled. He said, "It is a good thing we have these white jackets." The president got out and walked up to the man at the desk. The president said very loudly, "We are from the bug company. You called us about the bugs you have in this hotel."

"Shhhhhh," the man at the desk said. "Don't talk so loudly."

[1]

The president said, "The man who called us said the bridal rooms were full of bugs. Show me to the bridal rooms."

"Yes, yes," the man said. "But don't talk about bugs so loudly. I don't want any people to hear that we have bugs in this hotel."

"Private!" the president shouted. "Come in here and get to work."

So the con man came running into the hotel. And the desk man took the president and the con man to the bridal rooms. The president said, "This looks very bad. We will have to spray this room. You can't come in here for 24 hours."

"Yes, yes," the desk man said. "But please don't talk about bugs."

[2]

1 oul would could shouldn't

2 alarm whiskers charge leave
ordered sneak lunch while about

3 curls high right remember
suddenly nobody give wig
idea blinked rapped first
bride bridal company buzz
closet mirror sweets full
rolled enemy attacking love
snoring pretty shaved chair

The Con Man Becomes a Bride

The president and the con man were in the bridal rooms of a big hotel. The president had told the man at the desk that he and the con man were from the bug company. The president had said that somebody called about the bugs in the bridal rooms.

The president said, "This is the life." He sat down on the bed. "I need something to eat, private. Go down to the dining room and get a big lunch for us. Charge it to the room."

The con man said, "But I'm not—"

"Hush up, private," the president yelled.

"If you want to stay in this army, you must remember that I am in charge."

"Yes, sir," the con man said.

[2]

The con man went down to the dining room and ordered a big lunch for two. "Charge it to the bridal rooms," he said.

Then he went back to the bridal rooms. The president was sleeping on the bed. The con man said to himself, "I must get away from this guy, but I need a plan."

He sat in a chair and began to think. The president was in the bed, snoring and snoring. Then the con man jumped up. "I've got a good idea," he said.

[1]

The con man ran to the closet. He found a bridal dress in the closet. He said, "I will put this dress on. Then I will sneak from this hotel. Nobody will think that I am a con man. They will think that I am a bride."

So the con man slipped into the bridal dress. Then he shaved his whiskers. He looked at himself in the mirror.

"My hair is not right," the con man said. He went back to the closet and found a wig with big, black curls.

[1]

Just then the president rolled over in his sleep. He rolled right off the side of the bed. When he hit the floor, he jumped up. "Sound the alarm," he cried. "The enemy is attacking us."

Then the president saw the con man. He said, "Hello, there. I am President Washington. Who are you?"

The con man said in a high tone, "My name is Jane."

The president walked over to the con man. The president said, "My, but your dress is fine. And your hair is very pretty."

The con man smiled and said, "Tee, hee."

[2]

Suddenly, somebody rapped on the door. "Come in," the president said.

A woman came in with the lunch for two. She had hamburgers, pickles, corn chips, and cake.

The president said to the woman, "Give yourself a tip of five dollars. Just charge it to this room."

"Yes, sir," the woman said. She smiled and started to leave the room. Then she stopped and said to the con man, "What a sweet dress."

The con man said, "Buzz off."

The woman left and the president said, "Let's have a bite to eat, my dear."

The con man said, "Tee, hee."

So the con man and the president sat down to eat lunch in the bridal room.

[2]

1 ir

A	B
bird	shirt
thirst	dirt
first	sir

2 beard   trained   should   dash   army

loudly   leaving   ordered   buster

3 Valley Forge   hamburgers   junk

smell   bride   high   please

sniffed   ago   air   floor   attack

isn't   away   main   talking   winked

enemy   battle   striped   suddenly

money   sorry   behind   we've

4 # The Escape from the Hotel

The con man and the president were having lunch in the bridal room. The president said, "This room is a mess. I told that bum private to get lunch. But look at the junk he ordered. Hamburgers and cake. The army just isn't what it was years ago."

The con man said, "You are so right."

"Yes, my dear. Let me tell you about the battle that we had some years back. The enemy army had us holed up in a spot named Valley Forge. We were—"

Suddenly, the president stopped. He jumped up and sniffed the air. "I smell the enemy," he said. "They are going to attack. I know it. And I don't even have my army with me. Where is that private?"

[2]

The president ran to the window and looked down at the street. "There are cop cars down there. We must escape."

The president ran to the closet and came back with dress pants and a striped coat. He slipped into them. Then he cut some hair from the con man's wig and made a beard with it. He stuck the beard on his chin. Then he grabbed a top hat from the closet.

He looked at the con man and winked. "Don't think of me as the president," he said. "Think of me as a dashing man-about-town."

The con man said, "Well, let's dash, buster."

"Who said that?" the president asked.

"Who do you think, buster?" the con man said.

[2]

The president began to get red.

"Private," he yelled, "I don't think this is one bit funny. Now let's get out of here before the cops get us and send us back to that rest home."

The president and the con man went down to the main floor of the hotel. But, just as they got there, the cops came in the front door. The con man whispered, "We've had it now."

"Shut up, private," the president said. "Just stick with me."

[1]

The president walked over to the desk. "What kind of a hotel is this?" he said very loudly.

The man behind the desk blinked. "What is the matter?" he asked.

"The matter? I'll tell you what's the matter. THERE ARE BUGS IN OUR BRIDAL ROOMS. DO YOU THINK WE WOULD STAY IN A HOTEL WITH BUGS?"

"Shhhhhhhhhhhhhh," the man said. "Don't say anything about bugs."

"Don't say anything?" the president said. "I'll say EVERYTHING. THERE ARE BUGS IN THIS HOTEL."

"Please, please," the man said. "We will be glad to give you another room, any room you wish."

"No," the president said. "My bride and I are leaving. Give me my money back."

[2]

The man behind the desk said, "Yes, sir. Just how much money was that?"

"TWO HUNDRED DOLLARS," the president said, and he winked at the con man.

Very quickly, the man gave the president two hundred dollars. As he handed the money to the president, he said, "I'm very sorry about this. And if there is—"

"Let's go, my dear," the president said to the con man.

He grabbed the con man's hand. In his other hand he held two hundred dollars. The president and the con man walked past the cops. They went out the front door. They got into a cab, and they drove away.

[1]

1 ir

A	B
third	girl
shirt	first
bird	dirt

2 igh

A	B
high	light
right	night
fright	brightness

3

inches   afraid   marching

neared   beach   trench   chill

couldn't   bleet   louder

4

A	B
every	everything
any	anybody
some	something
no	nobody
her	herself
day	daytime

5

patrol   gasoline   month

barracks   millions   difference

animals   trumpet   coming

brap   wake   drams   brick

brabble   bubbling   seemed

remembered   moon   been

sky   planet   attacked   ago

6

Jean on Patrol

The night was cool. Jean looked up at the five moons in the night sky. "I will never feel at home on this planet," she said to herself. She was on night patrol. Her job was to patrol a strip that led from the beach of the red lake to the barracks. Nobody liked night patrol, not with the drams.

The drams were little animals that lived in the red lake. They looked like grasshoppers, but they were bigger. About three times a year, they came out of the lake. When they did, things got very bad. They ate everything in their path. They ate wood and bricks. They ate the yellow plants that lived on the planet.

[1]

Last year, they had eaten the barracks. Seven years before that, they had attacked some of the women who didn't get out of the barracks. Nobody could find a way to stop them. The drams moved like a big army, with millions and millions of drams marching and eating, marching and eating.

Jean had been on the planet for a little more than six months. She had seen the drams before. One night, they had come from the lake making that "bzzzzzz" that they make. Then they had made their way up the beach to the barracks, eating everything in their way.

[1]

Then the drams had stopped, just before they reached the barracks. They had stopped going "bzzzzzz." They had stopped marching. They had been still for nearly an hour. The women had run from the barracks.

Everybody watched the drams. But the drams seemed to be sleeping. Then the drams marched back to the lake. They went under water, and that was the last time anybody had seen them.

As Jean patrolled the strip to the beach, she kept thinking about the drams. Why had they stopped the way they did? What made them stop? And when were they coming back?

[1]

Jean began to think of the things that had happened the night that the drams stopped near the barracks. It was a hot night, but heat did not seem to make any difference to the drams. Three years ago, the women had made a trench and filled it with gasoline. They lit the gasoline, but it did not stop the drams. Drams kept piling into the trench. When the trench was filled with drams, more drams came—by the millions. They went to the barracks and attacked the women.

Jean remembered that the night was bright when the drams had stopped. But brightness hadn't stopped the drams in the past. When the women had trained spotlights on the drams, the light hadn't seemed to bother them.

[2]

There must have been something about that one night that made the difference, but what was it? Jean remembered that she had been on her way to the barracks when the drams started coming from the lake. She remembered how the women had yelled, "The drams! The drams! Let's get out of here." She remembered how some women ran to the barracks and began to wake up the other women.

Jean had been afraid. She had never seen anything like the drams before. But they had stopped. And Jean kept thinking that there was something that had made them stop.

[1]

As Jean neared the lake, she stopped and looked over the water. It looked like glass. At night, you couldn't see how red the water was, but in the daytime the water was bright red— nearly orange.

Jean felt a chill as she was standing near the shore of the lake. It was a big lake. It was so big that Jean couldn't see the other side. The brabble birds were not making their "brap, brap." Everything was still.

Jean was ready to patrol the strip back to the barracks when, suddenly, she heard something in the water. It was a bubbling sound near the shore. It became louder and louder. And then she saw them coming out of the water, going "bzzzzzz."

The drams.

[2]

1

igh

A   B

bright   sight
fright   light
high   moonlight

2

clearly   thousands   first
flash   couldn't   breathing
started   Carla

3

wall   move   few   remember
guy   other   soon   idea
month   major   meters   blow
melted   tried   skipping
silent   frozen   shiny
barracks   button   moment
messed   springs   stared
stayed   attacked   gasoline
fifty   patrol   pressed

The Drams Attack

For a moment, Jean was frozen as she looked at the drams coming from the lake. She could see them clearly in the moonlight. They were shiny as they moved up the beach.

For a moment, Jean didn't remember that she was to signal the barracks as soon as she spotted drams. She wanted to run—run as fast as she could go. She wanted to run as far from the drams as she could get. But she couldn't seem to move. She stared at the drams as they came closer and closer. They were only a few meters from her now.

[1]

"Move. Get out of here," she said to herself. But her legs felt as if they had melted.

Then Jean began to think. She reached for her signaler. She pressed the button. Lights began to flash in the barracks. Women began to yell, "The drams! The drams! Let's get out of here."

And Jean began to run. Now her legs felt like springs. Did she ever run! It was about three blocks from the beach to the barracks, and Jean ran to the barracks so fast that she felt as if she had run only a few meters.

[1]

When she got to the barracks, she ran up to the major. Jean was breathing very hard. "Major!" she said. "Major! Major!"

The major said, "Take it easy."

"Major," Jean said to her, "the drams are coming. They're coming. They're coming up the beach, and we've got to stop them. We've—"

"Take it easy," the major said. "Go stand with the women on the other side of the barracks. We'll take over. Just stay out of the way of the drams."

"Okay," Jean said, and she ran to the other side of the barracks near a grove of bleet trees. There were about fifty women standing there. One of them said, "Were you the one that spotted the drams?"

"Yes," Jean said. "They're coming! They're coming!" Jean's hands were shaking.

[1]

Another woman said, "Where is Carla? I haven't seen her."

Some of the women yelled, "Carla, where are you?" But Carla didn't call back.

"Is she in the barracks?" Jean asked.

"I don't know," one of the women said. "She sleeps like a log. Maybe she didn't hear the signal."

"I will go get her," Jean said.

"No," one of the women said. "You stay here. Don't go back into the barracks."

The women fell silent. Far off, Jean could hear the "bzzzzzz" of the drams. They were coming up the beach. Soon they would reach the barracks. If anybody was in those barracks, she would be attacked. If Carla was in the barracks—

[2]

Jean ran for the barracks. Some of the other women hollered, "Come back. You can't go in there."

But Jean kept running. She ran inside. "Carla, Carla," she yelled. "Carla, where are you?"

Jean ran to the far end of the barracks. Carla's bed was messed up, and her trumpet was on a table next to the bed. But Carla was not in her room.

"Carla!" Jean called. "Carla!"

[1]

Jean ran to some of the other rooms. Then she ran back to Carla's room. Then, suddenly, a sound came from the other end of the barracks. Crash!

Part of the wall fell down. Then another part fell down. The "bzzzzzz" of the drams became very loud. Jean could see them now— thousands of them, marching into the barracks.

"I've got to get out of here," she said to herself, "But I've got to find Carla," she said. "I can't leave Carla here with the drams coming."

Jean tried to think. Her legs wanted to run. But she kept thinking of Carla. And the drams were coming closer and closer.

[2]

1 al

A	B
all	almost
call	wall
fall	always

2

sight   streaming   sharp

cheek   would   right   eaten

3

A	B
her	herself
spot	spotlight
out	outside

4

off find air asleep middle

idea move few tried

swung wiggled still floor

alive trying report brave

even dumb every patrol

cliffs move turn

5

Trapped in the Barracks

The drams were at the other end of the barracks. They had eaten the wall, and now they were streaming over the floor. Jean was standing outside the door to Carla's room. Carla was not in sight. Jean had to get out of the barracks before the drams reached her. And she had to find Carla. The drams were coming closer. The "bzzzzzz" was very loud.

Jean ran into Carla's room. She grabbed the trumpet from Carla's table. "I can make a loud sound with this horn," Jean said to herself. She took in a lot of air. Then she pressed the trumpet to her lips.

"Brrrrrooooooooooooo," went the horn.

Suddenly the floor shifted. A crash came from the middle of the barracks. The drams were getting closer. "No time to blow the horn again," Jean said to herself. "I must get out of here."

She ran from Carla's room. A mass of drams was on the floor. Jean tried to run past them, but one dram got on her leg. It bit a hole in her pants. Jean tried to slap it off, and she tried to run at the same time. Another dram was on her back.

"Ow," Jean yelled. She slapped the dram and it fell to the floor. Five or six drams were on Jean now. One got on her cheek and bit her.

[1]

A sharp pain shot from her cheek. She hit the dram, and it fell to the floor.

[2]

Now there was a mass of drams on her. They were on her arms and her neck. They were on her legs and her back. She wiggled and tried to shake them off, but they were biting her.

She yelled, and kept running. She ran over piles of drams. She fell into a hole that they had made in the floor. She got out of the hole and began to run again. She swung her arms this way and that way. And she ran.

She ran from the barracks. Then she ran to where the women were standing. The women rushed up to her and began to swat the drams that were on her. Jean was crying and shaking. She couldn't stand still.

[1]

Two women held Jean while the others slapped the drams. Then one woman said, "These drams are sleeping. Look at them."

Jean looked. The woman was right. The drams were not eating. They were not going "bzzzzzz." They were hanging onto Jean, but they were very still.

The major ran up to Jean. She said, "What do you think you're doing. You're lucky to be alive. What made you go into the barracks?"

"I had to find Carla," Jean said.

The major said, "Carla is on patrol out near the cliffs. She's not in camp."

[1]

Jean looked down. One of the women said, "But look at the drams, major. They're asleep."

"Yes," another woman said. "Every dram is sleeping. They're not marching. They're just sleeping."

The major shook her head. "If that doesn't beat all," she said. "I wish I had some idea about what makes them sleep." Then she patted Jean on the back. "You did a brave thing," she said. "I'm going to have to report you for not following orders, but you did a very brave thing in trying to save Carla."

Jean looked up and said, "Thank you."

The women looked at the sleeping drams. They had made a big mess. They had eaten all the plants from the beach to the barracks. They had eaten nearly all of the barracks, even the windows. But now they were sleeping.

[2]

Suddenly a woman yelled, "More drams are coming." Three spotlights turned to the beach. Jean could see the drams. They had just come from the water, and they were starting up the beach.

The major said, "I wish I had some idea about how to stop them. But I don't know where to begin."

Jean tried to think. "Think," she said to herself. "Something made the drams go to sleep. Think about what happened. Think." Jean was still shaking, but she began to think of everything that had happened just before the drams went to sleep.

[1]

1

al

<u>A</u>   <u>B</u>

all   almost

fall   calling

wall   always

2

night   part   streaming   proud
breathed   blushing   would

3

beach   marching   pipe   crash   hour
pressed   months   deeply   water   forgot
forget   blowing   bitten   funny   blast
stunned   again   hungry   hunger   lined
buzzing   their   why   find   off

4

Stop the Drams

Jean was trying to think of everything that had happened just before the drams went to sleep. She remembered how she had been running with the drams biting her. She ran and fell into a hole in the floor. She remembered getting out of the hole and running again.

But were the drams biting her then? "Think, think."

"No," Jean said to herself. "I don't remember being bitten after I fell into the hole. Something must have happened before I fell into the hole."

Jean tried to think of everything that happened before she fell into the hole. She looked at the beach. More drams were marching closer to the barracks. They were marching over the sleeping drams. "Bzzzzzzzzzzz."

[2]

"Think, Jean. Think."

"I was running from Carla's room," Jean said. "My running couldn't make the drams go to sleep. It must have been something that happened before I ran. What did I do? What did I do?"

The drams were very close to the barracks now. "Bzzzzzzzzzzz."

Jean started to rub her cheek. She saw that she was still holding Carla's trumpet. "That's funny," she said to herself. "I forgot that I still had it. I must have held onto it when I ran from the barracks."

Some of the drams were streaming into the barracks now. "The horn," Jean said. "I gave a blast on Carla's horn. Maybe that's what stopped them."

[1]

Jean breathed in deeply. Again she pressed the horn to her lips. The horn let out a big blast. "Brrrroooooooo." The drams kept coming.

Part of the floor in the barracks gave way with a crash. Jean shook her head. "The horn doesn't work," she said. "I have to keep on thinking. I have to—"

Just then a woman yelled, "Look, the drams have stopped. They're sleeping."

"The horn did it," Jean yelled. "The horn stopped them." Some women began to slap Jean on the back.

[1]

"Good job," one of the women said. "What made you think the horn would stop them?"

"I don't know," Jean said. "I just kept thinking of everything that happened before they went to sleep."

After about an hour passed, the drams began to move again. But they didn't buzz or eat. They went back into the lake.

Now the women had a way to stop the drams, but they didn't know why the trumpet worked. Three months passed before the major told them why the trumpet worked the way it did.

[1]

"Thanks to Jean," the major said, "we know why the drams come out of the water. They are hungry. They are hungry for sound. They can't hear the kind of buzzing sound they hunger for when they are under water. So they come out of the water and buzz. They buzz until they have their fill of the sound. Then they go back to the water.

"The sound of the horn gives them their fill of sound very fast. It stuns them. When they are stunned, they seem to be sleeping. After they wake up, they go back to the water.

"They don't come out for another three months or so."

[1]

One of the women said, "Does that mean that we can stop them just by blowing horns when they come out of the water?"

"We can do better than that," the major said. "We can pipe sound into the lake. We can keep them from getting hungry for sound. If they don't get hungry for sound, they won't leave the lake."

The women smiled and looked at each other. Jean was thinking, "Now night patrol won't be so bad."

Then the major said, "I would like to thank the woman who showed us how to stop the drams—Jean Parker."

Jean could feel her cheeks blushing. But she was very proud—very proud.

[2]